LONDON TO PORTSMOUTH WATERWAY

P.A.L.VINE

MP Middleton Press

1994

First published November 1994

ISBN 1 873793 43 X

Design - Deborah Goodridge

Published by Middleton Press
             Easebourne Lane
             Midhurst
             West Sussex
             GU29 9AZ
             Tel: (0730) 813169
(From 16 April 1995 - (01730) 813169)

Printed & bound by Biddles Ltd,
             Guildford and Kings Lynn

CONTENTS

ACKNOWLEDGEMENTS

The following people very kindly lent or assisted with the location of illustrations:- Alan Bell, Peter Beresford, the Bodleian Library, Chiswick Public Library, Bob Dawes, Dendy Easton, Guildford Muniment Room, Matthew Alexander (Guildford Museum), Tony Harmsworth, Timothy Hudson, Peter Jebens, Mrs. Avril Lansdell, Littlehampton Museum, Mrs. Nellie Lofting, Hayward Madden, Vic Mitchell, Klaus Marx, Hugh McKnight, Oxford City Library, Portsmouth City Library, Fred Saigeman, Roger Sellman, Peter Taylor, Victoria Public Library, West Sussex County Record Office, West Sussex Institute of Higher Education (Bognor Regis), Ian Wright, John Wood and members of the Wey & Arun Canal Trust. The Tate Gallery has kindly allowed the reproduction of J.M.W. Turner's drawing of the river Arun. Kay Bowen prepared the typescript.

1841 advertisment

HISTORICAL BACKGROUND

Not many Londoners are aware that a century or so ago vessels sailed through Surrey and Sussex from the Thames to the English Channel. It was a circuitous trip. Barges, loaded at Queenhithe Wharf by Southwark Bridge, proceeded upstream past the House of Commons to Shepperton where they entered the Wey Navigation and were drawn by horses up to Guildford. This was a good spot to moor for the night and get some refreshment before continuing up the Godalming Navigation to join the Wey & Arun Junction Canal at Shalford. Another seven locks brought you to the five mile summit level at Cranleigh. It was now downhill all the way to the Arun Navigation and the junction with the Portsmouth & Arundel Canal at Ford or the sea at Littlehampton.

Compared to contemporary canals which linked great rivers like the Rhine and the Danube or the Thames and the Severn it was small beer. But it was not an easy route. The 115 mile journey to Portsmouth required the passage of 52 locks, a tow by tug from Chichester to Langstone Harbour and the payment of toll to six different companies. The canal suffered from a shortage of water, the tug *Egremont* had a weak boiler and the Arun was celebrated for its floods. Then there was the tunnel at Pulborough - the first and only tunnel to be built for a river navigation in Britain. To avoid a long bend in the river, the Arun proprietors had dug a short cut through the meadows and a 375 yard tunnel. It was less than twelve feet wide and without a tow-path. To pass through you had to lie on your back and push with your feet against the dripping brick arch. The horse, you hoped, would be waiting at the other end - that is if a reliable lad had been found to lead the animal over the hill.

This most extraordinary line of navigation was built by private enterprise in fits and starts. It took 175 years from the time the first parliamentary bill was introduced to its

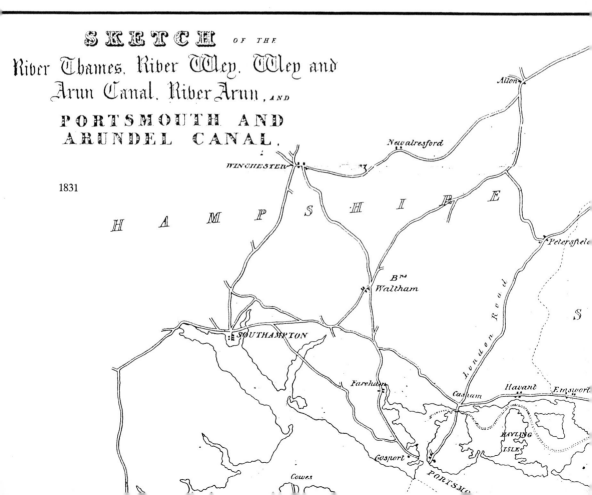

SKETCH OF THE

River Thames, River Wey, Wey and Arun Canal, River Arun, AND

PORTSMOUTH AND ARUNDEL CANAL.

1831

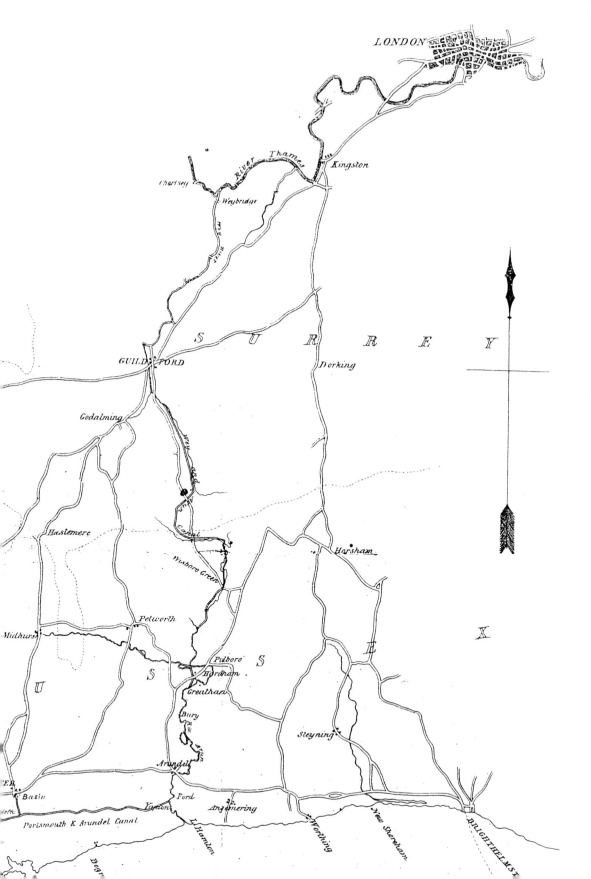

completion. The Wey Navigation reached Guildford in 1651 and was extended to Godalming in 1763. The river Arun had been improved up to Pulborough by 1600 and canalised as far as Newbridge in 1787. Nearly thirty years were to pass, however, before the through route could be completed and this achievement was largely due to the efforts and enthusiasm of the third earl of Egremont.

Lord Egremont is best known for his patronage of art and his ability to breed a winner or two. His Petworth stables produced five Derby victories but racing was really an amusement for his younger brother. His particular interests were agriculture and attractive women. His many children were all illegitimate but he appears to have loved them all, had many of them living at Petworth with their respective mothers and even hired a boat in September 1805 so that his family could see Nelson join the fleet at Portsmouth. In 1791 Egremont had obtained an Act of Parliament to build the Rother Navigation at his own expense and after it was completed, he planned to build a waterway from his estate at Petworth to Godalming. When he was thwarted in this venture, he subscribed one fifth of the capital for building the Wey & Arun Junction Canal.

The prospectus, drafted by Egremont himself, estimated local traffic at 30,000 tons and hoped that one twelfth, or 100,000 tons, of the London-Portsmouth trade would pass through the canal to avoid encounters with French privateers and the risk of shipwreck on the Goodwin Sands. The line involved the surmounting of few natural obstacles and digging commenced in July 1813 under the supervision of the engineer, Josias Jessop, (1781 - 1826) who was the second eldest of the eight children of William Jessop.

The opening of the Wey & Arun Junction Canal took place on 29 September 1816. By all accounts it was an inauspicious autumn day. Lord Egremont, accompanied by the Mayor and Aldermen of Guildford, assembled before the Compasses Inn at Alfold, where after providing a roasted ox and 200 gallons of ale for the "navigators", they embarked on four gaily decorated barges; accompanied by two bands and followed by a string of lighters loaded with coal and timber, they began the ten mile voyage to Guildford. The County Chronicle described the colourful scene from St Catherine's hill - "The sunshine which now broke out, combined with the unrivalled scenery of the favourite spot, the music, and numerous assemblage of spectators, and the merry peal of the bells at Guildford, Shalford and Godalming, all heard at this time, gave an effect to the scene which could not be contemplated but with the most lively and pleasing emotions".

After a civic welcome at Guildford, more than a hundred dined at a banquet given by the Company at the White Hart. "And thus", said the Times correspondent, "has opened under the happiest and most promising auspices, a canal, 18 miles in length, through a beautiful and picturesque country, to which it is as ornamental as it promises to be beneficial".

But although the price of coal fell by 13s a chaldron in Guildford, trade was slow to develop. The opening of the Portsmouth & Arundel canal seven years later in 1823 brought an initial increase in traffic, but that navigation was soon to prove a disastrous failure; in 1824, its most successful year, only 4000 tons, and not the hoped for 100,000, were carried between Portsmouth, Chichester and London. In 1827 ambitious plans to build a Suez size ship-canal from the Thames to Portsmouth also created much speculation but came to naught after John Rennie had estimated its cost at £6½ million.

Rennie considered the Arun Navigation to be very bad. Contemporary accounts tell of impositions by the bargemen, of piracy and delays due to ice, drought and floods which prevented passage through the tunnel and many of the bridges. Attempts at improvement were made. The central arch of fourteenth century Stopham Bridge was raised in 1822, the navigation was deepened, a tow-path built, but to little avail. The voyage from Portsmouth to London still took four days, often longer.

Trade was three times greater from London than from the Coast; coal and groceries, and in smaller quantities porter and pottery arrived regularly from the Thames, but consignments to the metropolis varied from timber, bark and hoops, to more unusual items like furniture, eggs, marble, soldier's baggage, and Indian cotton. Every month or so until 1838 precious cargoes of gold bullion guarded by red-coats passed through from Portsmouth bound for the Bank of England. One day in 1825, the *Union* and the *Portsea* went through together with 72 tons on board, but there are no reports of robbers being repelled in Glasshouse Copse. Manure and farm produce predominated the local traffic. Chalk and lime came from the Houghton pits and sometimes the *Lark* carried as much as 45 tons of sea-weed to Guildford. Though traffic had become negligible when an impetus was given to local trade towards the close of the 1830s by reducing the tolls, receipts rose by 30% between 1835 and 1840, but 23,000 tons was the most the Wey & Arun was ever destined to carry for the railway era had begun. Steam power was replacing that of sail, obviating the need for the safer but more costly inland passage.

Dividends never exceeded 1%. The toll on coal fell by a shilling a ton on the opening of the London - Guildford railway in 1845, after which dividends steadily declined as receipts dropped. Meanwhile the shares, which had cost their owners ££110 pounds, tumbled as soon as it became evident that the navigation was not a profitable undertaking. By 1820 they had fallen to half their nominal value and a decade later to a third; in 1850 they fetched a bare ten pounds. The opening of the Guildford - Horsham railway in 1865 attracted the bulk of the canal's remaining trade and the passing of an Abandonment Act in 1868 enabled it to be closed in the summer of 1871. The land was thereupon sold back to the riparian owners.

In spite of the closing of the connecting link, the Wey Navigation continued to carry commercial cargoes until 1983. Barge traffic also continued on the River Arun until the advent of the ubiquitous motor-lorry in the 1920s although pleasure boating on the river up to Pallingham has never ceased.

Further Reading:

A detailed account of the history of this line of navigation will be found in *London's Lost Route to the Sea* (David & Charles, 4th edition 1986) and London's Lost Route to Basingstoke (Alan Sutton, 1994). Additional illustrations will also be found in *West Sussex Waterways* (1985), *Surrey Waterways* (1987) and *Hampshire Waterways* (1990), all published by Middleton Press. All the aforementioned publications are by your present author.

1. Lord Egremont (1751-1837)

WHAT IS THERE TO SEE TODAY?

The best way to explore the former barge route is by boat from London Bridge to Shalford in Surrey and from Pallingham to Littlehampton in Sussex. The derelict canal sections between Shalford and Pallingham, between Hardham and Coldwaltham and between Ford and Birdham are best explored on foot. For a century the abandoned remains of these waterways became the haunt of flora and fauna. Countryside explorers rhapsodised on how nature had transformed the artifice of man into a thing of beauty and admired the swarth of yellow irises amongst the crumbling brickwork of the locks or decking the hulk of some forgotten barge. However, over the past twenty years the 850 or so members of the Wey & Arun Canal Trust, with the help of sympathetic landowners, have succeeded in clearing and dredging five miles of the canal bed, reconstructing seventeen bridges and restoring six of the twenty-three locks. The Hon. Secretary, John Wood (24 Griffiths Avenue, Lancing, West Sussex) welcomes new members to assist in completing this project. Enquiries regarding the Chichester Canal Society should be addressed to Edward Hill at 9 Marden Avenue, Chichester, West Sussex.

SUMMARY OF LINE OF DIRECT NAVIGATION BETWEEN

LONDON BRIDGE AND PORTSMOUTH HARBOUR

Waterway	From	To	Distance miles	N° locks	Year opened	Year regular commercial traffic ceased	Whether navigable (1994)
Thames Navigation	London Bridge	Shepperton	30	3(a)	(b)	partially in use	yes
Wey Navigation	Weybridge	Guildford	15 ¼	12	1653	1983 (c)	yes
Godalming Navigation	Guildford	Shalford	2	2	1763	1925	yes
Wey & Arun Junction Canal	Shalford	Newbridge	18 ½	23	1816	1871	no
Arun Canal	Newbridge	Pallingham	4 ½	3	1787	1888	no
Arun Navigation	Pallingham	Hardham	3	none	c1550	1905	yes
Coldwaltham Cut	Hardham	Coldwaltham	1 ¼	3	1790	1889	no (d)
Arun Navigation	Coldwaltham	Houghton	4	none	c1550	1930	yes
River Arun	Houghton	Ford	10 ½	none	c1550	1930	yes
Portsmouth & Arundel Canal Navigation	{Ford	Hunston (e)	9	2	1823	1847	no
	{Hunston	Birdham (f)	2 ½	2	1822	1906	partially
	{Birdham	Milton (g)	13	none	1822	1838	(j)
	{Milton	Portsea (h)	2 ½	2	1822	1825	no
	{Langstone Harbour	Portsmouth Harbour (i)	1	none	1830	1838	(j)

In 1831 the distance from London Bridge to Portsmouth Harbour by inland navigation was about 115 miles. By sea almost twice the distance.

- (a)   Richmond half tide lock was not opened until 1894.
- (b)   In use from time immemorial. Various types of weirs predated the building of pound locks at Teddington (1811), Molesey (1815) and Sunbury (1812).
- (c)   T&D Murrell revived commercial traffic from Tilbury to Coxes Mill Weybridge 1978 - 1983.
- (d)   The river Arun remains navigable between Hardham and Coldwaltham via Pulborough (5¼ miles).
- (e)   Barge canal.
- (f)   Part of Chichester Ship Canal.
- (g)   Dredged channel south of Thorney Island and north of Hayling Island.
- (h)   Portsea Ship Canal.
- (i)   Portcreek.
- (j)   At high tide only.

RIVER THAMES

2.   Tombleson's map of the Thames, 1830 showing the bridges the bargemen passed between London Bridge (marked nº 6) and Weybridge where barges bound for Guildford and Arundel entered the Wey Navigation.

Westminster Abbey	1
Dº Bridge	2
Waterloo Dº	3
Blackfriars Dº	4
Southwark Dº	5
London Dº	6
Custom House	7
Tower	8
Sᵗ Catharines Dock	9
Thames Tunnel	10

3.   London Bridge as it appeared in 1756 shortly before the demolition of the houses. In spite of the City Corporation carrying out improvements suggested by John Smeaton in 1761, by the time of the opening of the inland water route through Surrey and Sussex in 1816 the bridge remained a serious hazard. Every year numerous watermen and bargemen were injured or drowned when their boats capsized while trying to pass under the arches against the rushing tide or strong current.

4.   The next London Bridge was designed by John Rennie and completed by his son Sir John Rennie.   Opened in 1831, the overhanging granite corbels were added at the turn of the century to widen the bridge but Rennie's original entablature survives and can be seen above the arch which crosses Thames Street. Fearnside commented in 1834 that immediately on passing the bridge downstream could be seen the picturesque ruins of the old bridge. (See bottom right).

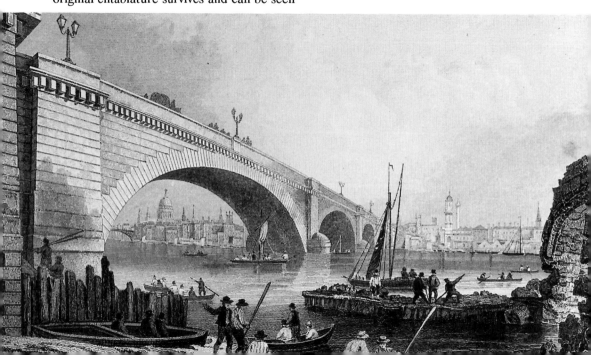

5. Southwark Bridge, looking upstream, is seen from the numerous wharves and warehouses along Bankside in 1827. The bridge was designed by John Rennie and opened in 1819. It was greatly admired for its "stupendous" iron arches whose centre span measured 240 feet.

The 1875 map has Queenhithe Wharf on the left and Southwark Bridge on the right.

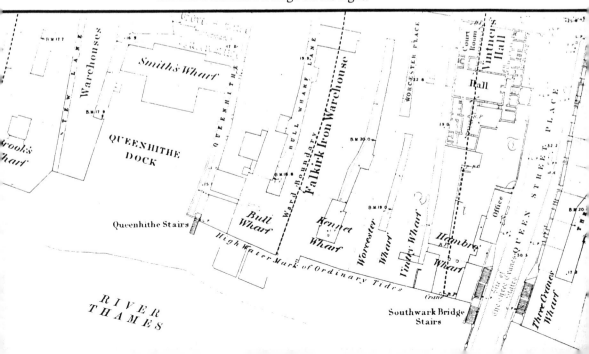

6. Southwark Bridge looking downstream in 1834. This view of Southwark Bridge and St. Saviours Church was drawn looking downstream in 1834. It shows the scene at Brook's Wharf by Queenhithe whence the London & Portsmouth fly barges departed every Saturday in the 1830s. This bridge was replaced in 1920, St. Saviours having become Southwark Cathedral in 1905.

PORTSMOUTH AND LONDON
FLY BARGES,
EVERY SATURDAY,
From BROOK'S WHARF, Upper Thames-Street.

M⁰ ⸻⸻⸻⸻⸻⸻⸻⸻

To Freight from London, by Fly Barge,
of 10 November 1831 ⸻

1 Cask,	1.14		0	2	6
26ᵗʰ December					
2 Hampers 0.3.4			0	1	6
			£ 0	4	0

JOSEPH PUSHMAN, Agent.
OFFICE—OYSTER-STREET, PORTSMOUTH.

7. The wharves adjacent to Queenhithe, depicted here in 1851, were frequently advertised as points of dispatch for goods to Arundel and Chichester. Seward & Co's barges left Chichester and Arundel two or three times a week bound for Queenhithe while those of Richard Isemonger left Littlehampton every Monday for Three Cranes Wharf. The Hampshire Telegraph reported in June 1823 that the Portsmouth & Arundel Navigation Company's Fly Barge reached Queenhithe from Portsmouth in 2 days 16 hours and made the return journey in 2 days 20 hours. It was pointed out that these times could be improved since there had been a delay in getting horses and some had had to be used which had previously done their day's work.

8. Queenhithe Wharf is seen from Southwark Bridge in 1855.

9. A tug lowers its chimney to pass under Southwark Bridge in 1938. Queenhithe Wharf is in line with St. Pauls Cathedral.

10. Blackfriars Bridge in 1792. It had been opened in 1769 after the approach to the bridge over the Fleet Ditch had been arched over. This bridge was replaced in 1864.

11.   Waterloo Bridge - 'the finest bridge in Europe' - was designed by John Rennie and opened in 1817. In this 1827 view a hay barge is being unloaded. When London's streets were full of horse drawn traffic most of the hay required to feed the horses came by fleets of barges with twelve feet of hay stacked on their decks working up the river. The longevity of some barges was amazing. *The Defiance*, a 40 ton barge built at Maidstone in 1789, was employed in stack work in her later days and continued trading until 1928. The trade lasted until the 1930s. The stone bridge with its nine elliptical arches was demolished in 1937 and replaced by the present reinforced concrete structure.

12. Hungerford Bridge was built by Isambard Brunel and opened in 1845. The bridge was demolished to make way for Charing Cross railway bridge in 1863 and the chains moved to the Clifton Suspension Bridge where they now span the River Avon. The building of the Victoria Embankment between Westminster and Blackfriars bridges (1864 - 1870) caused the wharves at Scotland Yard to be obliterated and also allowed the construction of the main interception sewer which prevented foul water from entering the Thames. Previously, as this 1850s picture indicates, lighters unloaded groups of moored hay boats, distinguished by their brilliantly painted hulls and brightly coloured sails. Barges also conveyed fruit and vegetables to Hungerford Market until it disappeared when Charing Cross station was built.

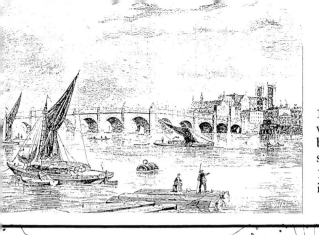

13. Westminster Bridge, seen here in 1754, was opened in 1759 to replace the ferry. It was built of Portland stone and had 13 large and 2 small arches. The bridge which replaced it in 1862 is double its width and built chiefly of iron.

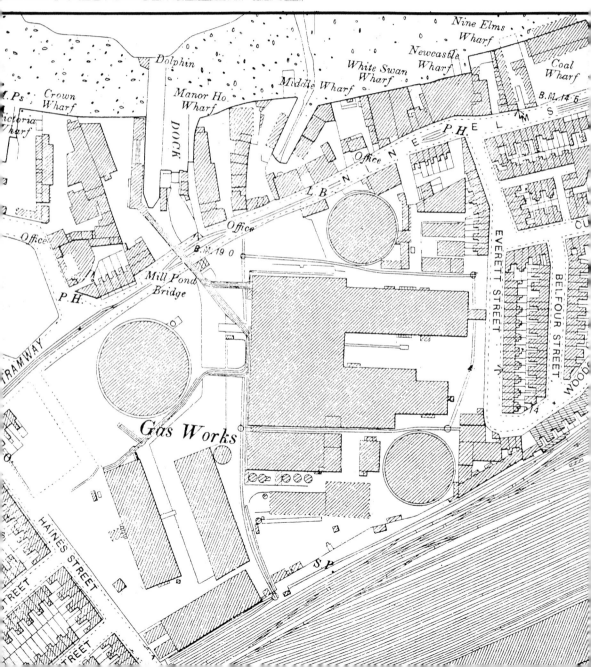

RIVER
THAMES

Railway
W'harf

L &
Instit

Brunswick Y
(L & S.W.R

e Elms
er

Mud

14

14

L. B.

Offices

harves

Engine
H.

P. H.

P. H.

P. H.

Brewery

12

Smy.

Sch.

N E

Nine Elms Goods Depôt
(L & S. W. Ry.)

B.M. 15.4

E L M S

R
O
A
D

Instit

B.N.
12.0

WORTH

WY

S. B.

S.P.

S.B.

STREET

STREET

The London & Southampton Railway
established its London terminus at Nine Elms
in 1838 and development of an extensive
wharfage soon followed. Not only did this
allow for interchange of freight traffic, but
passengers continued their journeys to the
West End or the city by barge until the
extension of the railway to Waterloo in 1848.
The gasworks on the left of this 1895 map
received its coal by barge.

Stores

B.M.
.13.0

Grosvenor Canal lock and the new disinfecting station, 1910.

The Grosvenor Canal was opened in 1823 from the Thames just below Chelsea Bridge to a basin, occupied since 1860 by the Grosvenor Hotel and an extension of Victoria station. The canal was extensively reconstructed in 1929 and is currently used by Westminster City Council to barge away refuse. The entrance channel lies between the railway bridge and Chelsea Bridge (right) on this 1869 map.

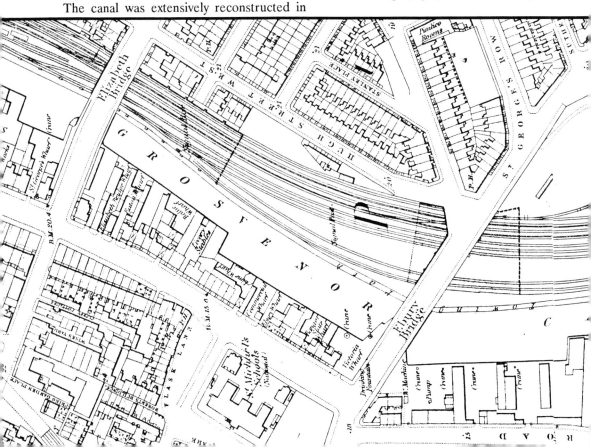

14. Grosvenor Road crosses the entrance to the Grosvenor Canal downstream from Chelsea Suspension Bridge. This view was taken in 1928.

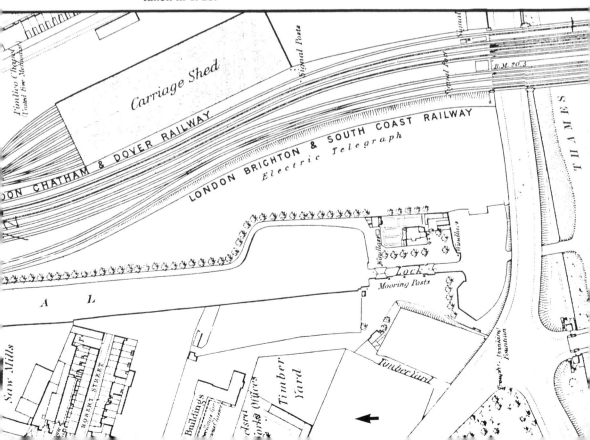

Grosvenor Canal entrance basin from
Chelsea Bridge Road, 1910.

15.   The bowler hatted lock-keeper seen
working the entrance lock to the Grosvenor
Canal at Pimlico, 1885. The spacious
lock-house contained 4 bedrooms and there
were 2 flats for engineering staff on the second
floor.

Extensive wharfage was created upstream
from Battersea Bridge and on Chelsea Creek,
shown at the top of this 1916 edition. Most
traffic in this creek was coal to Lots Road
Power Station (top centre) where the
electricity for the London Underground is still
generated. Chelsea Basin (lower centre) and
the sidings were built by the Great Western
Railway for exchange of freight traffic. The line
at the bottom of the map crosses the Thames
to Clapham Junction.

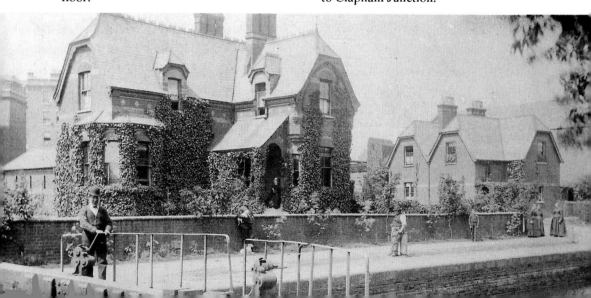

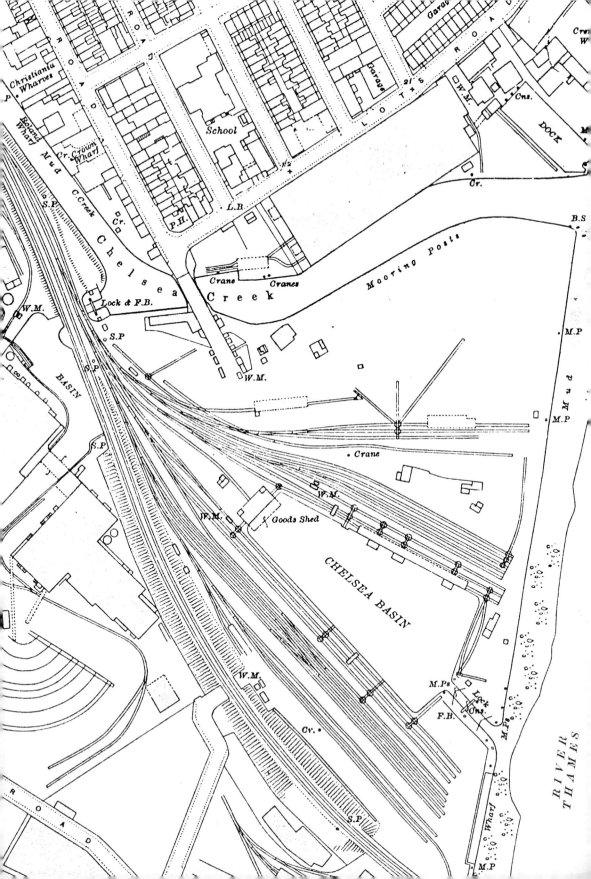

16. Nineteenth century view of Chelsea Hospital from Battersea Fields. The hospital was founded by Charles II for aged and disabled soldiers. Battersea Fields was a dreary locality until Battersea Park was opened in 1858.

17. Hammersmith's first iron suspension bridge, depicted here, was opened in 1827. The bridge was replaced by a new suspension bridge designed by W.T.Clarke in the 1890s.

18. For much of the nineteenth century Putney had a picturesque timber bridge, seen here in 1875, which was one of the last wooden structures to span the Thames. Built in 1729 upon piles, its openings were very small and a hazard to navigation. Ireland described it in 1792 as "decayed and tottering, which cannot fail to disgust the observer". It was not, however, until 1872 that an iron girder was inserted to provide a wider centre span for navigation. The old bridge was removed in 1886 after the opening of the present five arched granite structure.

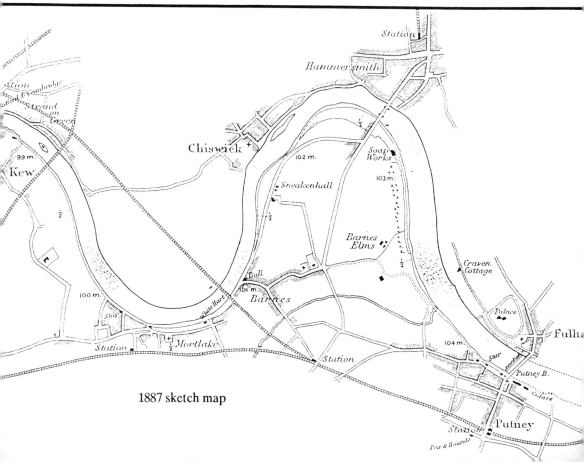

1887 sketch map

19. The aqueduct of the Chelsea Waterworks stood just above Putney bridge and was demolished when the new bridge was begun in 1882. Fulham church is in the background.

20. The *Maria Wood* was recorded lying at Fulham in 1875. Built in 1816 for "the occasional pleasurable summer excursions of the Lord Mayor, The Corporation and their Guests", eight horses were required to tow the state barge upstream, two or three down. Her winter quarters were at the old Barge House at Lambeth. After the establishment of the Thames Conservancy in 1857, she passed into the hands of various owners. In 1881 she was moved from her old berth at Kew to Isleworth Ait. In 1897 Punch recorded that she was up for sale there 'enjoying the osiers cum dignitate'.

21. An 1878 view of Strand on the Green includes the chimney at the end of Kew Bridge which forms part of the pumping station of the Grand Junction Waterworks, later to become the Metropolitan Water Board. The works now houses an impressive steam museum.

22. This is the same view as no. 21 but seventy years later. The modern block to the left of the old chimney was built for Simmonds Aerocessories in the 1930s. After the war it became the offices of BOAC and in 1955 was taken over by Beechams.

23. Kew Bridge 1893. The first bridge, opened in 1759, was replaced by this stone one in 1789. This bridge was replaced by the current one in 1903, when its opening was celebrated by a banquet held in marquees erected above the arches.

24.   This view from Kew Bridge of *Jane of Rochester* at Strand on the Green was recorded in about 1905.

25. The Grand Junction Canal was opened in 1793 from Braunston to the Thames at Brentford. This 1893 view shows the original gauging lock (nº 100) at Brentford. The lock was duplicated in 1900 and the waterway became part of the Grand Union Canal in 1929. Henry Taunt, the Oxford photographer and author of guide books to the Thames, commented in 1887 that Brentford dock was "often very animated when a large number of boats are waiting for the tide to flow, and, although in their cups sometimes bargemen are quarrelsome, yet ordinarily they are quite as good-natured and obliging as the majority of the working classes".

26. Wooden lighters laden with coal are waiting to be unloaded at Brentford Gas Works in 1926. Those in the foreground were used to remove rubbish.

The GWR's first freight interchange depot was established at the mouth of the River Brent at Brentford. This 1935 map shows a covered transfer shed (left of centre) and the last lock on the Grand Union Canal above it. Lower right is part of Kew Gardens to and from which people of high office once travelled by barge in connection with the royal palace there.

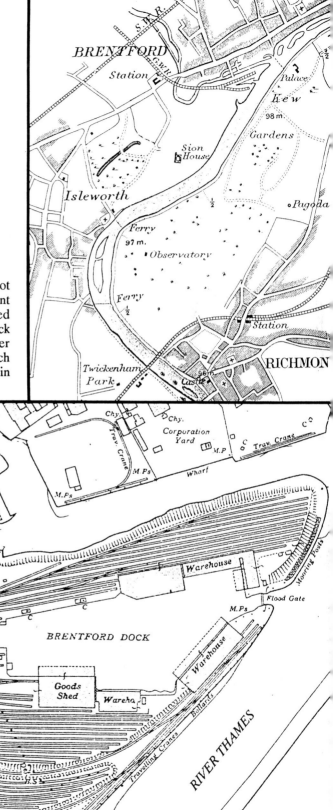

27. Richmond Bridge is seen in about 1830. It was designed by James Payne and opened in 1777. It was described in 1779 as consisting of "13 arches, 8 of which are brick and the other 5 handsomely built of stone. These have stone balustrades on each side, but the five arches of brick on the Middlesex side have only wooden palisades. That part of the bridge over the three brick arches on the Surrey side has, for the security of passengers, a brick parapet wall on each side capped with stone. The interior parts of these three arches are converted to private uses: one being a storehouse, the second a stable, and the third a stone-mason's workshop".

28. Twickenham wharf viewed from Eel Pie Island in 1883. A coal barge is waiting to be unloaded.

29. The first full lock on the Thames at Teddington was nearly 19 miles upstream of Queenhithe. The 1810 Act authorised the building of four pound locks and allowed barges to draw 3ft 3ins from May to October and 3ft 10ins for the remainder of the year. The first pound lock at Teddington, seen here in 1834, was opened for river traffic on 20 June 1811. Prior to the opening barges frequently grounded on the shallows.

30. Until the Thames Conservancy was set up in 1857, the City of London had jurisdiction over the River Thames from London Bridge to Staines. Teddington Lock had been rebuilt in 1858 and in 1872, when this view was taken, a boatslide (at right) in front of the moored barge had been introduced for skiffs and canoes.

31. A later view of Teddington Lock taken in 1883 nineteen years before the double lock was opened. Nowadays the central of the present locks measures 650 feet long, 25 feet wide and is fitted with three sets of gates capable of taking a tug and its tow of six barges at one time; the other locks are 177 ft x 25ft and 50ft x 6ft. The footbridge across the river was not completed until 1888.

32. The Anglers' Hotel, Teddington, 1883. In 1878 it advertised that the present proprietresses, the Misses Kemp and Mrs. Jacob, "having made extensive alterations, including a Billiard Room, they are enabled to offer increased accommodation and amusement to Gentlemen Fishing and Rowing up the River. Private and public sitting rooms commanding a good view of the river. Well-aired beds. N.B. No connection with the Beer-shop kept by Mrs. William Kemp". Next door (in centre of picture) was the Albion boat-house owned by Pocock, a "practical boat, punt and canoe builder" who also repaired gentlemen's boats on their own estates.

33. Cargo is waiting to be unloaded at Kingston Wharf in 1870, with Kingston Bridge, opened in 1828, in the background. In 1846 the parking of carts and waggons under one of the arches led to complaints that at night they were "tenanted by vagabonds and people of the worst description". The bridge was widened in 1914 from 25 to 55 feet between the parapets.

River T[hames]

Boat House

Boat House

Boat House

Landing Stage

M.P.

M.P.

Sewage Works
(Kingston upon Thames Corporation)

22

W.M.

W.M.

Allotme[nt]
Garden[s]

W.M.

Electricity Works
(Kingston upon Thames Corporation)

S.P.

F.F.

Kingston Bridge

M.Ps

Wharf
Trav.
Crane

S.P.

S.B.

S.P.

Boat House

Down Hall

The 1913 survey indicates the importance of Kingston as a pleasure and commercial boating centre. The Hampton Court Gas Company unloaded large quantities of coal on the west bank until a railway siding was provided at its works in Hampton Wick. A similar story applied to the local gasworks (top right). The electricity works (top centre) remained faithful to water transport, this also applying to the new works built after World War II. The tannery (lower left) generated water traffic and an awful smell in the town. Note the location of Old Bridge Street.

Landing Stages

Bath

M.Ps

Wharf

Mud

Wharf

Mortuary

Public Baths

Inft. Sch.

Hall

School

Buckland's Wharf

Boat House

Bridge Wharf

THAMES SIDE

OLD BRIDGE ST.

P.H.

P.H.

HORSE FAIR

P.H.

WOOD STREET

Kingston Bridge

37

Urinal

29

P.H.

Bh.

P.H.

CLARENCE STREET

M.Ps

THAMES STREET

Slip

Boat House

Bishop's Palace
(Site of)

Tannery

BISHOP'S HALL

F.B.

Grave Yd.

All Saints' Church
(Vicarage)

St. Mary's Chap.
(Site of)

P.H.

P.H.

L.B.

CHURCH STREET

Burial Ground

Baptist Church

Sun. Sch.

M.P

Landing Stage

Bh.

Miles	TIME TABLE OF STEAMERS KINGSTON TO OXFORD WEEK DAYS AND SUNDAYS	a.m.	a.m.	a.m.	a.m.	p.m.
—	Kingston Pier d.	...	...	...	9 0	2 30
15	Staines (Town Hall Steps) d.	...	...	...	11 50	5 25
22	Windsor { a.	...	...	...	1B30 *(p.m.)*	7 0
	Bridge { d.	...	...	9 30	2 45	...
29¾	Boulter's Lock (for Maidenhead) ... d.	...	...	10 45	4 20	...
31½	Cookham Lock d.	...	...	11 15	4 50	...
36	Marlow Lock d.	...	...	12 5 *(p.m.)*	5 40	...
44	Henley { a.	...	...	1A45	7 10	...
	Bridge { d.	...	9 10	2 45	...	...
47½	Shiplake Lock d.	...	9 45	3 25	...	...
53	Reading (Caversham Lock) d.	...	10 50	4 25	...	...
60	Whitchurch Lock (for Pangbourne) ... d.	...	12 0 noon	5 40	...	...
64	Goring Lock d.	...	12 40	6 20	...	...
70	Wallingford { a.	...	1A45	7 15	...	...
	Bridge { d.	9 0	2 45	...	...	...
78	Clifton Lock (for Culham Stn) d.	10 30	4 15	...	...	...
81	Culham Lock d.	11 5	4 50	...	...	...
83½	Abingdon ... d.	11 30	5 15	...	...	...
91	Oxford (Folly Bridge) ... a.	1 10 *(p.m.)*	7 0	...	...	...

Miles	TIME TABLE OF STEAMERS OXFORD TO KINGSTON WEEK DAYS AND SUNDAYS	a.m.	a.m.	a.m.	a.m.	p.m.
—	Oxford (Folly Bridge) ... d.	...	...	...	9 30	2 30
7½	Abingdon ... d.	...	...	...	11 0	4 0
10	Culham Lock d.	...	...	...	11 30	4 30
13	Clifton Lock (for Culham Stn.) d.	...	...	...	12 5 *(p.m.)*	5 0
21	Wallingford { a.	...	...	...	1C40	6 30
	Bridge { d.	...	...	9 0	2 45	...
27	Goring Lock d.	...	...	10 0	3 40	...
31	Whitchurch Lock (for Pangbourne) ... d.	...	...	10 40	4 20	...
38	Reading (Caversham Lock) d.	...	...	11 45	5 25	...
43½	Shiplake Lock d.	...	...	12 45 *(p.m.)*	6 25	...
47	Henley { a.	...	...	1B30	7 0	...
	Bridge { d.	...	9 45	2 45	...	...
55	Marlow Lock d.	...	11 5	4 15	...	...
59¼	Cookham Lock d.	...	11 45	5 0	...	...
61¼	Boulter's Lock (for Maidenhead) ... d.	...	12 15 *(p.m.)*	5 30	...	...
69	Windsor { a.	...	1B30	6 50	...	...
	Bridge { d.	9 20	2 45	...	...	...
76	Staines (Town Hall Steps) d.	10 40	4 10	...	...	...
91	Kingston ... a.	1 30 *(p.m.)*	7 0	...	...	...

A—One hour allowed for lunch.   B—75 minutes allowed for lunch.
C—65 minutes allowed for lunch.

34. The Swan Hotel, Thames Ditton established 1593 claimed in 1878 that it was one of the "most comfortable and beautifully situated houses on the river Thames between Kingston and Hampton Court Bridges". It offered "wines, spirits and ales of the very best description at moderate charges". It also had a spacious billiard saloon fitted with two first-class tables. This 1883 view shows both the hotel and the billiard saloon. Note the steamer moored to the opposite bank.

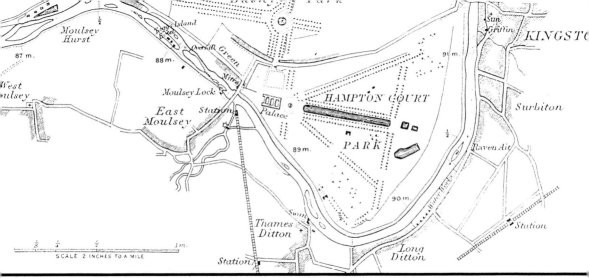

Taunt's sketch map of 1887 spells Molesey and Bushey Park incorrectly. Other sections letter the railways wrongly.

Salters steamers operated a frequent local service from Kingston Pier. This timetable for May to September 1951 shows their long distance trips on which return trips could be made by British Rail. Passengers could join or leave at most locks.

35.   The wooden bridge at Hampton Court was built in 1753. Barge masters complained regularly about the hazard, when proceeding downstream, of navigating the small central arch depicted here in 1792.

The "Swan", snug Inn, good fare affords,
As table e'er was put on,
And worthy quite of grander boards
Its poultry, fish, and mutton:
And while sound wine mine host supplies,
With beer in best condition,
Mine hostess with expressive eyes
Invites a stay at Ditton.

Let swells resort
to Hampton Court,
Or happy Hampton flit on,
Or higher go
Up Thames - but oh!
Give me the "Swan" at Ditton.

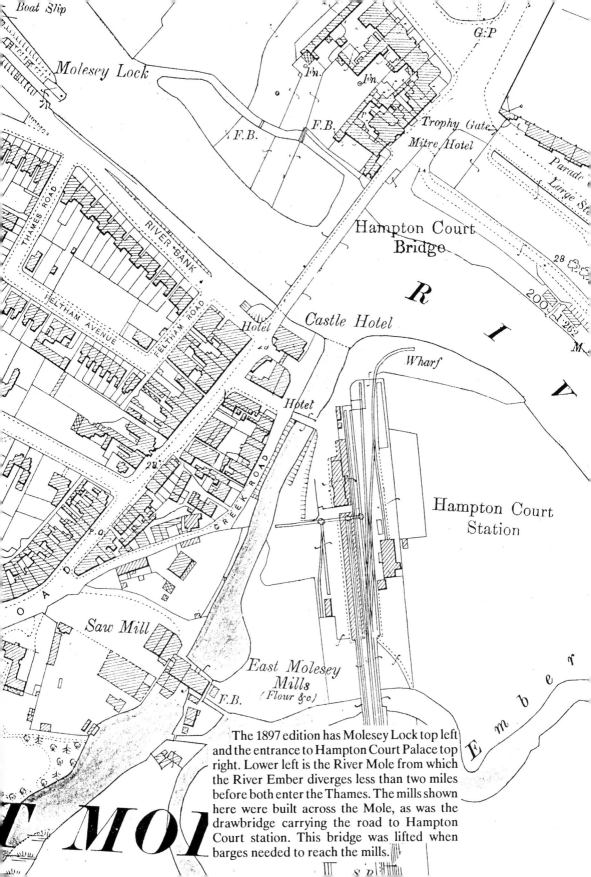

Boat Slip

Molesey Lock

G.P

Inn.

Inn.

F.B.

F.B.

Trophy Gate

Mitre Hotel

Parade

Large St

THAMES ROAD

RIVER BANK

FELTHAM ROAD

FELTHAM AVENUE

Hampton Court
Bridge

28

200

263

Hotel

Castle Hotel

R

I

V

Wharf

Hotel

M

28

CREEK ROAD

P.O.

Hampton Court
Station

Saw Mill

East Molesey
Mills
(Flour &c.)

F.B.

The 1897 edition has Molesey Lock top left
and the entrance to Hampton Court Palace top
right. Lower left is the River Mole from which
the River Ember diverges less than two miles
before both enter the Thames. The mills shown
here were built across the Mole, as was the
drawbridge carrying the road to Hampton
Court station. This bridge was lifted when
barges needed to reach the mills.

T MO1

Ember

S.P

36. The narrow approach to Hampton Court Bridge as viewed in 1834. The River Mole enters the Thames to the left of "The Castle" which had to be demolished to make way for the present road bridge in 1933.

37. Not until 1866 was Hampton Court bridge replaced by the five arched iron structure, seen here in 1878, with the milllls in the background. The present bridge was opened in 1933. It has three spans and the brickwork is faced to harmonize with Hampton Court Palace.

38. The first pound lock was opened for traffic at Molesey in 1815, the date being inscribed on the front of the Italianate style lock-house. The lock, seen here in 1883, was partially rebuilt in 1853 as a result of the reduced draught due to the extraction of water by the Hampton waterworks: the lock was not completely rebuilt until 1906 when it became the second largest on the river.

39. In the 1880s Molesey Lock was a most popular boating spot. Jerome K. Jerome wrote that when looking down into the lock from the quay, the scene formed one of the gayest sights near "dull old London town". This boating scene was recorded in 1895.

40. Molesey Weir 1880. Fish ladders had been added in 1864 and the weir was rebuilt in 1883.

41. The boat slide, built in the summer of 1871, is in use at Molesey Lock in 1883. St Mary's Church at Hampton is in the background.

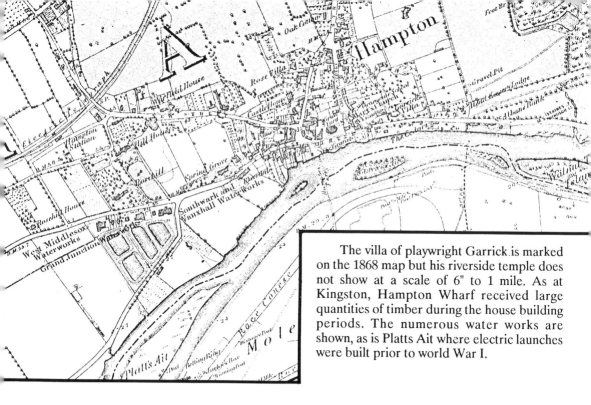

The villa of playwright Garrick is marked on the 1868 map but his riverside temple does not show at a scale of 6" to 1 mile. As at Kingston, Hampton Wharf received large quantities of timber during the house building periods. The numerous water works are shown, as is Platts Ait where electric launches were built prior to world War I.

42. The coal bunker (left), the railway wagons (right) and the Thames barges (not present) handled massive tonnages of coal until the works went over to electric pumps after World War II. The works was the biggest single user of this part of the Thames until then.

The Grand Junction Water Works Co. established works at Chelsea in 1820 and Kew Bridge in 1835, and supplied an area from Mayfair westwards. The Southwark & Vauxhall Water Co. was formed in 1845 and had a works at Battersea, which supplied South London as far as Nunhead.. In 1852, the Metropolis Water Act prohibited the abstraction of Thames water below Teddington Lock, which resulted in these companies building new works at Hampton. In 1902 they came under the control of the Metropolitan Water Board whose programme of improvements included the provision of a 2ft gauge railway between the works at Kempton Park and Hampton, with a line to their coal bunkers at the wharf on the Thames. The line was opened in 1915 and three identical 0-4-2Ts were built by Kerr, Stuart & Co. (nos. 2366-2368) to work the line. A new works, with steam turbines and coal conveyors, was opened in 1936 and the railway closed within a few years.

43. A sailing barge is passing downstream through Sunbury Lock in about 1830. The lock had been built in 1812 to replace a weir made of planks piled across part of the channel. Both the lock-house and the lock were rebuilt in 1856. In 1878 Taunt complained that the latter was very slow in emptying but that there was a boat-launch for small boats.

44. Sunbury lock-house as seen by Henry Taunt, in 1878. Taunt noticed that nearby were the breeding ponds for supplying the Thames with trout and that the river-keeper who lived close by would explain their "peculiarities".

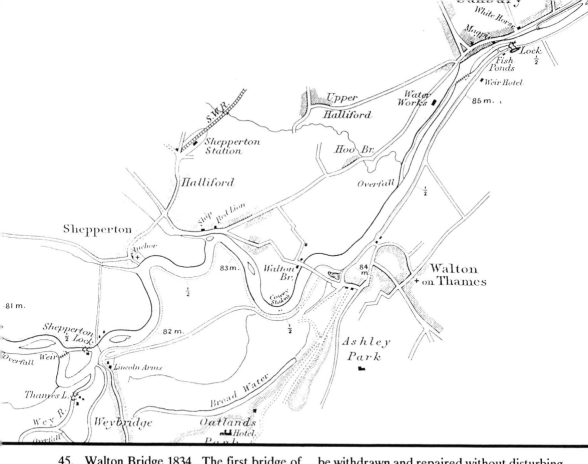

45. Walton Bridge 1834. The first bridge of three wooden arches was opened in 1750. It was a curious structure composed of timbers tangent to a circle of 100 feet diameter which had the advantage that any one timber could be withdrawn and repaired without disturbing the rest of the bridge. Rebuilt in the 1780s with the four large arches turned with stone and fifteen small brick arches over the flood plain, it was replaced by the present bridge in 1864.

WEY NAVIGATION

The River Wey was made navigable from its junction with the Thames at Weybridge to Guildford under an Act of 1671. The initiative had been taken by Sir Richard Weston of Sutton Place in the 1630s when he had erected a pound lock at Stoke but further work had to be postponed until after the end of the Civil War. Although the navigation was completed in 1653 at a cost of £15,000, tiresome disputes over compensation and ownership nearly closed the waterway in the 1670s. After these had finally been settled, barge traffic rapidly increased and Guildford prospered as it supplied the London markets with agricultural produce and a host of manufactured items which included beer, flour, paper and wooden goods. Daniel Defoe remarked in 1724 that the navigation was a mighty support to the corn-market at Farnham and that timber came not only from the neighbourhood but from the woody parts of Sussex and Hampshire, thirty miles away. For that decade annual tolls averaged £200 and the tonnage around 17,000. By 1800 this had increased to £5860 and 57,500 tons, a figure which was surpassed after the opening of the Wey & Arun Junction Canal (1816) by a peak of £7763 and 86,003 tons in 1838. Thereafter improved road transport and the coming of the railway (it reached Guildford in 1845) saw traffic gradually decrease, eg:-

1860	£3001	60707 tons
1870	£2083	41585 tons
1880	£1549	29414 tons
1890	£1136	24581 tons
1900	£896	28297 tons

There was then a minor revival which saw tolls reaching £1981 in 1927 (55,622 tons) and £1398 in 1948 (25,334 tons). However the collapse of traffic on the Basingstoke Canal coupled with the decline of traffic to the London Docks and the flexibility and increased carrying power of road transport finally caused commercial traffic to cease in July 1969. An attempt was made by T.D. Murrell to revive the grain trade to Coxes Mill, but this ceased when the mill was closed in April 1983. Ownership of the navigation is now in the hands of the National Trust who are encouraging pleasure boating and are able to maintain the waterway from revenue generated by land and mooring rents, visitors passes and annual licence fees which nowadays replace lock tolls.

46. Barges going upstream from London entered the Wey Navigation shortly before Shepperton Lock. Horse towage was used on the Wey Navigation until 1960. This scene depicts barges lying at the oil mills (at right) above Thames Lock, Weybridge. Linseed was brought up from the Thames until the mill was destroyed by fire in 1963.

47. This 1867 drawing indicates the difficulty experienced in working the Wey Navigation Locks. Normally the paddles (hatches) of a lock can be drawn by standing on a wooden platform and easing up the ratchets with a key. However, on the Wey it was necessary to climb on the lock-gate itself and winch up the paddle while balancing on the gate. A contemporary boater wrote "These hatches are always very stiff and difficult to raise and lower, and as it is necessary to get a good leverage, the crowbar must be worked from the extreme end of the handle, and if, whilst the wrench is made, the point should slip out of the niche into which it is placed, away goes the unfortunate being into the water".

48. A 1940s picture shows two Clydesdale horses working in tandem as they approach Blackboys Bridge, Addlestone on the last leg of their journey from London Docks to Coxes Mill, Weybridge.

49. Coxes Mill, Weybridge in 1953. Regular cargoes of grain were brought by barge to this flour mill from London Docks until July 1969.

50. The water-borne trade was revived by T & D Murrell in July 1978 using initially two narrow boats and in 1980 a former River Nene stone barge *Clinton* which could carry up to 70 tons from Tilbury without transhipment. In the autumn of 1980, the 34 ton *Anny* from Newbury was carrying 60 tons of grain from Tilbury, twice a week. In 1982 over 7,000 tons were carried but in April 1983 the milling operations at Coxes were closed down and transferred to tax-advantaged Corby.

51. Cart Bridge, Send was recorded in about 1910. Nearby was the residence and workshop of the Wey Navigation's master carpenter which stood by Worsfold Gates Lock.

NOTICE.

In consequence of several additional
Rates of Toll, and other Regulations
ordered by the PROPRIETORS of the
RIVER WEY, to take place on Barges
navigating the said River on the 1st of
July next, *a Meeting of the Timber,
Corn, and Coal Merchants, Iron-
mongers, Grocers, Barge Owners,
and others,* having Business on the
said Canal, is requested to be held at
the WHITE HART INN, GUILDFORD,
on SATURDAY the 24th of JUNE, at
three o'clock in the afternoon, to take
the same Regulations, &c. into their
consideration, and to consider the
propriety of establishing a **LAND
CONVEYANCE** between *Weybridge,
Guildford,* and *Godalming,* and to
adopt such Measures as the said
Meeting may think proper.

JUNE 23, 1826.   [RUSSELL, PRINTER.]

52. Triggs Lock still had turfed sides (as in the 17th century) instead of walls when photographed in 1960.

53. A laden Thames barge approaches Guildford in 1842. The Pewley Hill semaphore which formed part of the Admiralty's London to Portsmouth telegraph system can be seen at top left. It was in use from 1822 to 1847. The house remains occupied and is known today as Semaphore House. In favourable conditions a short message took about 15 minutes to pass the whole distance.

RIVER WEY, SURREY.--Mrs _Sparkes & Co_ account of Riverage, for one Quarter ending the 2⁴ of Sep⁰ 1873					
Places where Loaded and Unloaded.	No. of Loads.	At per Load.	£.	S.	D.
(No?) Godalming - - - -	11	1-6	11	6	6
Do.	16	2-0	1	12	
Guildford - - - -	87	4-6	19	11	6
Dapdon - - - - -		4-8			
Stoke - - - - -	183	4-0	36	12	-
Bowers - - - - -		3-0			
Triggs - - - - -	5	2-6		12	6
Send Heath - - -	6	2-6		15	-
Newark - - - - -		2-0			
Pyrford - - - - -		1-6			
Byfleet - - - - -		1-6			
Newhaw - - - - -		1-0			
Coxes - - - - -		1-0			
Weybridge - - - -		0-6			
			76	9	6
This Bill to be Paid by the 16 Oct 1873	Fares at 10s. 6d.				
Russells' Guildford Press.	Ballance £				

54.   Seen in about 1870, a sailing barge is
moored at Guildford Wharf. William Stevens
the barge owner and wharfinger had his office
here.   On the right are the offices of T.
Lethbridge, barge owner and coal merchant;
then comes Elkins' coal wharf where there was
also a brewery. Beyond lies the tread-wheel
crane 18 feet in diameter used to load sacks of
grain.

THE GODALMING NAVIGATION

The Wey Navigation Act (1760) extended the waterway 4½ miles from Guildford to Godalming. Four locks were built and an extensive wharf was developed at Godalming. During the American War of Independence considerable amounts of government stores were brought down from London to Godalming by water and carried from there by land to Portsmouth. Another important item was the carriage of gun- powder brought by waggon from the Chilworth powder mills to Stonebridge Wharf, Shalford. After the closure of the mills in 1921, only two barges reguarly worked the river between the two world wars. Godalming Wharf ceased to be used in 1925, commercial traffic above Guildford ceased in 1950 and in 1969 the navigation was handed over to the National Trust. It is now regularly used by pleasure craft.

55. Guildford Bridge as it appeared in 1754. The medieval bridge had to be rebuilt when the Wey Navigation Act of 1760 authorised the extension of the waterway to Godalming.

56. Guildford Town Bridge in the 1860s. The right hand arch is part of the original medieval bridge rebuilt in 1762. The alteration attracted unfavourable comment. One writer referred to it in 1828 as "one of the clumsiest pieces of architecture that ever disgraced a civilised place of residence" and went on to remark that the widening of the bridge with iron arches in 1825, as depicted here, had produced a "graceful and durable structure". However

during the great floods in February 1900 timber from Moon's yard blocked the arches and caused the bridge to collapse. The bridge which stands today was opened in 1902.

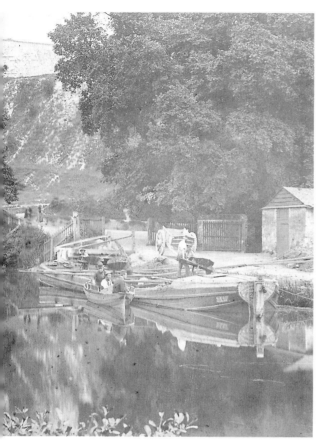

57. Loading chalk from the immense Guildford Quarry into George Davis' barge at Davis' wharf in around 1870. John Davis had leased two chalk pits from the Wey & Arun Junction Canal Company in 1821. Cargoes of chalk were carried down the Wey & Arun as far as Elm Bridge Wharf, Cranleigh while the kilns beyond were served from the pits in Sussex.

58. A sailing barge on the Godalming Navigation approaches St Catherine's Ferry near Guildford. Water-colour by W.F.Varley in 1819.

59. Stonebridge Wharf, Shalford in 1865. The wooden building on the right housed the wooden tread-wheel crane, which was used, amongst other things, to load gunpowder brought by cart from the Chilworth Powder Mills. The powder was barged down the Wey to the Thames and the magazine at Barking Creek. In the 1830s cargoes totalled about 100 tons a year which increased to 300 tons during the Crimea War and in 1873 exceeded 500 tons. In August 1864 a newly delivered barge - the last to be built at the Pallingham boatyard - belonging to Samuel Sharpe of Chilworth, had been loaded with gunpowder at Stonebridge wharf, and was only a mile or so from the wharf when it exploded. The two men on board were blown to pieces and the vessel sank. These dangerous cargoes continued to be carried by water to the magazines at Woolwich, Purfleet, and Barking Creek until 1921.

The Chilworth Gunpowder Company. Limited.			
FREIGHT per Barge 'Kate' to Royal Arsenal, Woolwich.		CHILWORTH. 23 - 12 - 1914	
POWDER.	HOW PACKED.	SHIPPING MARK.	TOTAL. lbs.
M.D. Cordite.			
Lots B 549 & 553 Size 8	144 Cases.		10080
„ B 550 & 556 „ 4¼	134 „		10050
Mrs I Cordite			
Lot B. 554 Size 20	144 „ Also 3 bags of packing pieces.		10,080
	For the Deputy Director of Ordnance Stores, Royal Arsenal.		30210

WEY & ARUN JUNCTION CANAL

The Wey & Arun Junction Canal linked the Wey Navigation at Shalford with the Arun Canal at Newbridge near Wisborough Green thus providing an inland water route from the Thames at Weybridge to the English Channel at Littlehampton. Although an attempt to link the rivers Wey and Arun had been made in 1641 the Parliamentary bill failed to pass through the House of Lords (see London's Lost Route to the Sea chapter III) and it was not until 1813 that an Act of Parliament was obtained. The canal was surveyed by Josias Jessop, a son of William Jessop and constructed first by Zachariel Keppel, a local contractor of Alfold who went bankrupt and then completed by May Upton, the Petworth surveyor.

The canal was opened for traffic on 29 September 1816. Its total length was 18½ miles and the main engineering works consisted of 18 locks, over 30 bridges and two small aqueducts at Bramley and Drungewick. Besides serving the villages of Bramley, Wonersh, Cranleigh, Alfold, Dunsfold and Loxwood, it formed the only inland water link between the Thames and the English Channel.

The cost of building the canal was £107,000; £99,550 was raised by the issue of 905 shares of £100 at £110 each and the balance by mortgaging the tolls. The largest shareholder was George O'Brien Wyndham, the 3rd Earl of Egremont who held 250 shares or 28 per cent of the equity. The highest dividend paid on the £100 shares was 1%; the last of 6/- per cent was distributed in May 1866.

Barges from the coast brought seaweed for the farms, grain for the watermills, coal for the gasworks and a wide variety of groceries and merchandise for the village stores; they returned loaded with bark, farm produce, flour, forest timber and items like hoops and the other products of rural industry. Local traffic consisted mainly of chalk, clay, sand and gravel from the pits to the kilns and wharves at villages and farms. Exceptionally, the waterway from Portsmouth to London saw barges guarded by red coats carrying bullion to the Bank of England; more frequent were the cargoes of eggs, wine, old rope, rags and soldiers' baggage. Occasionally their manifest showed oddities like acorns, bullock horns, burr stones, carrots, cyder and fruit.

The tonnage carried was never substantial. It averaged only 9,000 tons until the opening of the Portsmouth & Arundel Canal in 1823 when it rose to an average of 16,000 tons during the next seven years.

In spite of the virtual demise of the London to Portsmouth trade the average exceeded 18,500 tons during the 1830's. Although the peak tonnage of 23,250 in 1839–40 was never surpassed, it did not drop below 10,000 tons until after the opening of the Guildford-Horsham Railway in 1865. An Act of Abandonment was obtained after much difficulty in 1868 which allowed the canal to be officially closed on 22 July 1871.

Barges however continued to trade to Bramley Wharf until 27 June 1872. The land and buildings belonging to the canal company were gradually sold back to the riparian owners.

Although many writers and countryside explorers have bewailed the loss of this waterway over the past eighty years, serious efforts to reopen the canal only began in 1970 with the formation of The Wey & Arun Canal Society, later to become the Wey & Arun Canal Trust. It now has 700 members and has successfully raised money through sponsored walks, jumble sales and from donations. The Trust has been responsible for clearing and dredging five miles of the canal bed, putting Rowner and Mallam locks back into working order and rebuilding numerous bridges and culverts. The Shalford Natural History Society cleared and repaired Tanyard Bridge at Gosden in 1977. Similarly the Pulborough Society was among those who contributed to the cost of rebuilding Pallingham Quay Bridge which was re-opened in 1976. Before the line of the former waterway can be restored however, formidable difficulties remain to be overcome since some landowners who now own some 13 miles of the canal bed do not wish a public right of way to divide their land. The fact that a large housing estate has been built upon the canal bed at Bramley will also necessitate a new line of waterway being cut. The prospects for the navigation being fully restored are therefore uncertain. Much will depend on the results of a cost feasibility study currently being undertaken, the attitude of the Surrey and West Sussex County Councils, the Southern Water Authority, the forty or so riparian landowners and the continued enthusiasm of the many voluntary workers who have already been toiling amidst the undergrowth and mire for more than a decade.

60. The first bridge over the Wey & Arun Junction Canal at Shalford is seen in 1952. The stream here was widened and dredged in 1815 and the canal itself dug from Stonebridge (which was rebuilt in brick) to Newbridge, Wisborough Green, a distance of 18 miles. The bridge which carries the Guildford to Horsham main road (A281) was replaced by a culvert when realignment took place in the late 1970s.

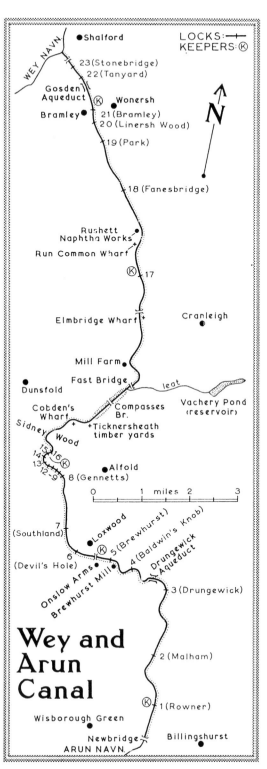

LOCKS:⊢
KEEPERS:Ⓚ

WEY NAVN

●Shalford

23 (Stonebridge)
22 (Tanyard)

Gosden
Aqueduct Ⓚ ●Wonersh

Bramley● 21 (Bramley)
20 (Linersh Wood)

19 (Park)

18 (Fanesbridge)

N

Rushett
Naphtha Works ●

Run Common Wharf

Ⓚ 17

Elmbridge Wharf   Cranleigh
                                 ●

Mill Farm●

Fast Bridge●
Dunsfold   leat   Vachery Pond
●   (reservoir)
Cobden's   Compasses
Wharf ●   Br.
Sidney Wood +Ticknersheath
              timber yards
15 16 Ⓚ
14
13   ●Alfold
12 9 8 (Gennetts)

0   1   miles 2   3

7
(Southland)   ●Loxwood 5 (Brewhurst)
                  Ⓚ   4 (Baldwin's Knob)
6   Drungewick
(Devil's Hole) Onslow Arms● Aqueduct
              Brewhurst Mill● 3 (Drungewick)

**Wey and
Arun
Canal**   2 (Malham)

Ⓚ 1 (Rowner)

Wisborough Green
●

Newbridge
ARUN NAVN.   Billingshurst
                  ●

61.   This is the approach to the site of Stonebridge Lock in 1952. The foot bridges link the gardens of the private residences which are divided by the old canal.

62.   The bridge over the canal at Gosden Common, Bramley. When the Guildford to Horsham railway was opened in 1865 the road bridge over the railway was extended over the canal (far parapet) and incorporated the canal bridge, built in 1815, to enable horses to cross from one side of the tow-path to the other. The Shalford Conservation Society restored the brickwork and cleared the heavily overgrown site. Here the author (left) is seen taking part in the reopening ceremony held in October 1977.

63. Gosden Aqueduct crossed the Bramley Stream immediately to the south of Tanyard Lock. The former Guildford-Horsham railway is in the background. The brick aqueduct seen here in 1952 was the first to be built to carry a canal in Surrey. The channel between Summersbury Tannery and the lock was filled in before 1895.

64. Here is a 1953 view of the canal at Birtley Farm, Bramley. After eighty years the derelict canal had become a haven of tranquillity, the haunt of coot and moorhen with reaches of charm and solitary splendour, the placid surface of the water hemmed with water weed.

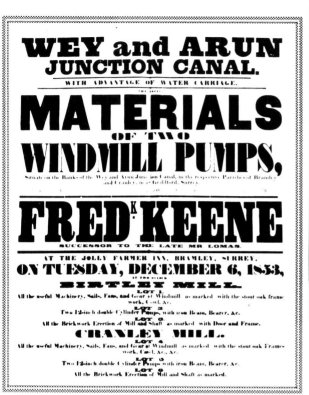

Vachery Pond was used as the 40 acre reservoir for the Wey & Arun Junction Canal. A two mile feeder conduit fed the summit level through a culvert south of Fastbridge.

The 2½" to 1 mile map shows the long meandering watercourse from the Vachery Pond to the canal.

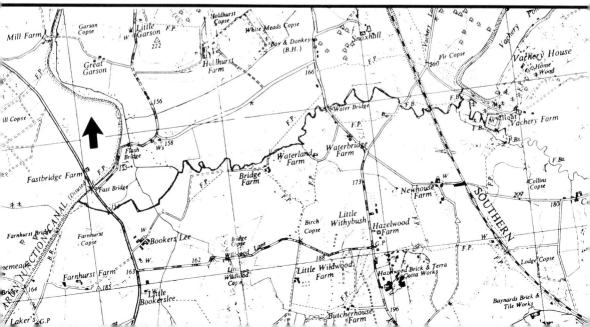

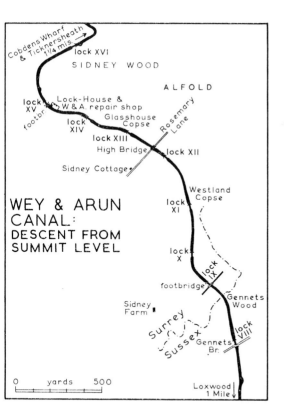

Cobdens Wharf & Ticknersheath 1¼ mis

lock XVI

SIDNEY WOOD

ALFOLD

lock XV

Lock-House & W & A. repair shop

footbr.

Glasshouse Copse

lock XIV

Rosemary Lane

lock XIII

High Bridge

lock XII

Sidney Cottage

Westland Copse

lock XI

WEY & ARUN CANAL:
DESCENT FROM
SUMMIT LEVEL

lock X

lock IX

footbridge

Sidney Farm

Surrey

Sussex

Gennets Br.

Gennets Wood

lock VIII

0   yards   500

Loxwood 1 Mile

WEY & ARUN NAVIGATION.
£5 REWARD

WHEREAS, on Sunday the 13th day of August instant, a quantity of the COPING on ELM BRIDGE was maliciously removed and injured;

NOTICE IS HEREBY GIVEN, that any Person who will give Information to Mr. STANTON, the Superintendent of the Navigation, so as to lead to the Conviction of the Offender or Offenders, shall receive a Reward of £5.

W. HAYDON SMALLPEICE, CLERK.

Guildford, 26th August, 1848.

Stramelin, Printers and Stationers.

65. Until the Wey & Arun Canal Trust began restoring locks in the nineteen seventies, most of the brick built locks had been plundered for their bricks. This picture shows Southland Lock near Ifold being demolished in about 1930. Note the thickness of the lock chamber walls.

66. The Onslow Arms at Loxwood, in 1963. Back in 1857 the Oarman's Guide drew attention to this canal side inn with its "three beds or so". Meetings of the Wey & Arun Canal Trust are now regularly held here and work is currently in progress to restore nearby Brewhurst Lock.

67. Brewhurst Lock, Loxwood in 1952. Although the canal had been disused since 1871 the lock gates remained standing until the late 1970s.

68. The Wey & Arun Canal Trust's trip boat was launched into the canal at Barnshill Bridge Drungewick in May 1994. Baldwin's Knob Lock has been rebuilt and the trust intends to operate a pleasure boat service from Loxwood to Newbridge as soon as Drungewick aqueduct has been rebuilt. It is hoped that this will be achieved within the next few years.

69. Drungewick Aqueduct carried the canal over the western branch of the River Arun. In 1934, in spite of being neglected for over sixty years, it remained relatively intact. It had three low flat arches and a solid parapet of red brick, the arches rimmed with four tiers of brick and the parapet capped with white stone. Only the left arch was beginning to collapse but the north side, which had lost part of the parapet, was much in decay.

70. Eighteen years later the aqueduct was in ruins and the autumn floods of 1952 swept away the remaining arches as this 1955 view shows. The dry bed of the canal is clearly visible on the left.

71. The chamber of Drungewick Lock, built of blocks of Pulborough stone in 1815 is seen criss-crossed with fallen trees during the winter of 1963. The lock has now been restored by the Wey & Arun Canal Trust.

72. The canal bridge at Newbridge, built in 1814, carries the A272 and is seen in 1953. The tow-path passed beneath the bridge on the right hand side.

ARUN CANAL

The River Arun was made navigable to Stopham Bridge during the reign of Queen Elizabeth I. By 1637 barges could reach Pallingham Quay. The Arun Navigation Act, 1785 enabled the Arun Canal to be built to Newbridge and for the five miles of twisting river between Greatham and Pulborough to be avoided by means of the Coldwaltham cut which was carried beneath Hardham Hill and the London road by means of a 375 yard long tunnel. The cost of the canal and the tunnel was the substantial sum of £16,000.

The opening of the Wey & Arun and the Portsmouth & Arundel canals enabled improvements to be made to the navigation in the early 1820's. Consequently traffic increased from 17,600 tons in 1810 to 26,500 tons in 1824 and 36,000 tons in 1839.

The opening of the railways to Petworth (1859) and Arundel (1863) and the closure of the Wey & Arun Junction Canal in 1871 caused trade to drop from 20,000 tons in 1860 to 10,000 tons in 1870 and 5,000 tons in 1885. The Arun Canal was closed in 1888 but barge traffic continued to use the tideway until the late nineteen twenties, the Strudwicks of Fittleworth, the Doicks of Pulborough and the Henlys of Bury being the last barge-masters on the navigation.

73. In 1874 the Arun Navigation Company ceased to act as wharfingers at Newbridge and George Dunkerton who lived at the wharf house took on the responsibility until the end of 1885 when the company could no longer afford to pay his weekly wage. This photograph, from about 1885 is the only one known of barges berthed on the canal and shows his sons Frederick and Walter posing by two apparently derelict barges below the bridge. In 1888 the last craft passed up the canal to Newbridge and the navigation was closed. The bridge carries the main Billingshurst to Wisborough Green road (A272).

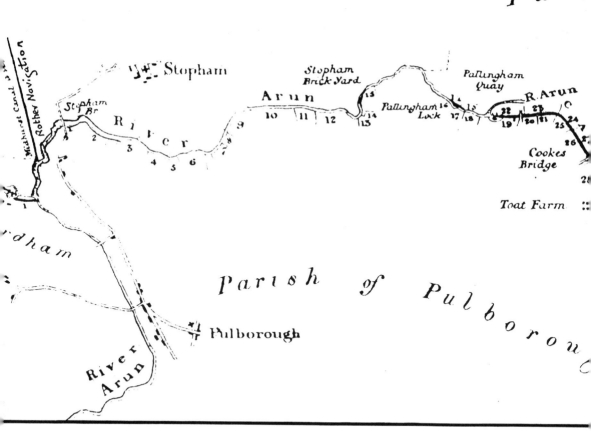

Midhurst Canal or Rother Navigation

Stopham

Stopham Brick Yard

Pallingham Quay

Stopham Br

R. Arun

Arun

R i v e r

Pallingham Lock

Cookes Bridge

Toat Farm

Parish of Pulborou

dham

River Arun

Pulborough

74.   Newbridge Wharf, the terminus of the Arun Navigation. In August 1823 William Cobbett passed by "Soon after quitting Billingshurst", he wrote, "I crossed the river Arun, which has a canal running alongside of it.   At this there are large timber and coal yards, and kilns for lime.   This appears to be a grand receiving and distributing place". Billingshurst and the surrounding farms and villages looked to the wharf at Newbridge for the arrival of their coal and groceries, for their fertilizers and fancy goods from London, Guildford and Arundel and as the most convenient means of dispatching their own wares and farm produce to market. The warehouse built in 1839 also served as the counting house of the navigation. Here the superintendent of the navigation had his office. Richard Seward held this position between 1826 and 1856 when the Arun proprietors "in recognition of his thirty years service and of his being liable to an increased income tax" increased his salary. After the navigation was closed in 1888, the building was used as a barn. Until the 1930s ledgers recording the barges'

manifest were still kept there. In 1986 it was purchased by David Mitchell who has converted it into a guest house and retained some of the old machinery used for hoisting water borne merchandise to the upper floor. The east elevation of the warehouse was photographed in January 1963 when the ice across the canal was several inches thick.

J.Hollinsworth Plan of the Arun Navigation in 1820 from Stopham to Newbridge.

75. Orfold aqueduct carried the canal over the River Arun. This 1964 photograph shows two of the three arches and the remains of the northern wall. A water wheel built in 1787 raised water from the river for the canal. The foundations of the adjacent lock-house can still be traced where in July 1867 J.B.Dashwood commented on "the lock-keeper's wife and two pretty daughters making butter in the early morn".

76. The entrance to Pallingham Lock was photographed in about 1918. The lock cottage was from 1792 always occupied by a member of the Stone family. James Stone was lock-keeper for 39 years and his son Benjamin Stone, who had been appointed lock-keeper in 1871, lived there until his death on 31 August 1935. Stone had a carpenter's shed and his wife Annie ran a bakery and grocery shop by the adjacent docks. The mooring posts are clearly visible as well as the pleasure boat used by Ben Stone, seen wearing his black hat.

77. A 1952 view of Stopham Bridge includes the White Hart. The bridge was built during the reign of Edward III. In the seventeenth century a drawbridge facilitated the passage of boats. In 1822 the central arch was raised to allow more heavily laden barges to pass.

78. Horses towing barges had to cross the River Arun at Stopham by this wooden "gallows" bridge i.e. a flat beam high above the water with an inclined plane on each side. This 1889 view shows Hardham Mill in the background. A red iron bridge replaced the wooden bridge in about 1914.

➡️

79. Hardham Lock 1889. It was here that 22 years earlier Mrs Dashwood (of pleasure boating fame) nearly came to grief when Dashwood's una boat *Caprice* drifted under an iron footbridge which crossed the lock. Barges coming down from London passed beneath Stopham Bridge and near to the entrance to the Rother Navigation before entering the River Rother. The lock at Hardham Mill enabled boats bound for Portsmouth to enter the Arun Canal and pass through Hardham Tunnel. The toll was 1s (5p) a ton but it saved the extra 3½ miles entailed in passing along the tidal river past Pulborough where shallows could be a problem.

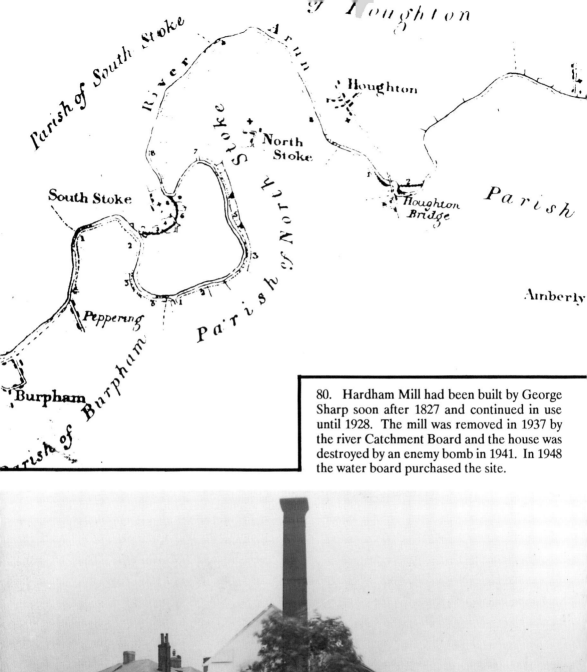

Parish of South Stoke

River Arun

Parish of South Stoke

North Stoke

Houghton

Houghton

South Stoke

Houghton
Bridge

Parish

Stoke

Parish of North

Amberly

Peppering

Parish of Burpham

Burpham

Parish of

80. Hardham Mill had been built by George Sharp soon after 1827 and continued in use until 1928. The mill was removed in 1937 by the river Catchment Board and the house was destroyed by an enemy bomb in 1941. In 1948 the water board purchased the site.

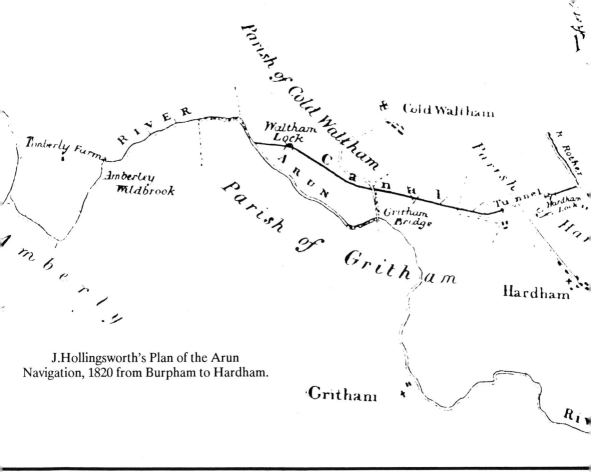

J.Hollingsworth's Plan of the Arun
Navigation, 1820 from Burpham to Hardham.

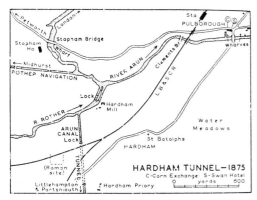

HARDHAM TUNNEL—1875
C-Corn Exchange S-Swan Hotel
0   yards   600

81.   The lock-house is seen from Hardham
Mill 1934. The latter was demolished by the
water authority in 1957 and the lock-chamber
was filled in.

82. Canal tunnels there were in plenty but Hardham Tunnel is unique in being the only one in Great Britain to have been used to avoid the bends of a river navigation. In Europe they are found on the Saone and other rivers. The Dashwood family passed through the tunnel in 1867 by punting their boat along by means of the boat-hook against the roof. "In the middle it became quite dark and we could only just guide ourselves by means of the bright outlet at the end. The roof was covered with stalactites, and in places the water fell upon us from crevices above in heavy drops, so that we had to try and steer clear of them where we heard their splash on the water below". This view, taken in 1951, reveals the north entrance to Hardham Tunnel which was opened in 1790 and last used in 1889. The dam was built by the water authority on the site of Tunnel Lock in 1952. Note the state of preservation of one of the lock beams which had formed part of one of the gates. The tunnel was blocked beneath the railway lines in 1898. The entrance to the brick underpass for horses, which was built when the Pulborough - Petworth railway was opened in 1859, was to the left side of the tunnel.

83. The ruins of Coldwaltham lock-house are seen in 1950. Picture 98 in *West Sussex Waterways* showed it as it was in 1941. By 1959 only a few bricks remained. The entrance to the Hardham tunnel cut was blocked by the water authority building a flood bank in 1970.

84.   A 1983 view of Greatham Bridge (18th century). After floods had swept away part of the bridge on 30 November 1838, the iron section was inserted to allow barges bound for Pulborough and London greater headroom.

85.   Sam Strudwick steers *Reliance* below Greatham Bridge, in 1913. For eighteen years he worked the river between Pulborough and Arundel. In 1923 he sold the barge to the Arun Brick Company which failed the following year and in July 1925 the Harbour Master at Littlehampton reported that the brick company had agreed to accept the abandoned *Reliance* in return for its removal from the tideway.

86. Ferryman Bob Dudden and his wife were pictured in 1931. The ferry closed in 1957. Amberley chalk pits, in the background, are now the location of a 32-acre craft and industrial history museum. The ferry closed in 1957.

87.   This 1889 view from Amberley Wharf includes Bury Church. Barges often brought up bolts of reeds and osiers from Burpham or Stoke for Pepper & Son at Amberley and were then moored beyond the wharf to await cargoes of chalk for the lime kilns along the Rother and the upper reaches of the Arun.

88.   The chalk pit behind Amberley Station looking east is seen in about 1904. In front is the 350 yard cut built by Lord Egremont in 1802 - 3 to enable barges to load chalk more easily. The cut was used in conjunction with the railway (opened in 1863) and was maintained until the outbreak of war in 1914.

89. The Black Rabbit Inn at Offham was originally a row of cottages. It has been a popular riverside pub since the turn of the century with rowing skiffs and gigs for hire. The chalk quarry at the rear was begun when the Offham Cut was made in 1861 - 2 and was in use until the nineteen seventies. This c1900 view shows the Arun Catchment Board's barge which carried up to 40 tons of chalk blocks to locations on the Arun whenever bank works were in progress.

90. A 1948 view of the Arun River Board barge, the *Swanbourne*, built at David Hillyard's shipyard at Littlehampton shows it leaving the Black Rabbit chalk pit at Offham near Arundel crewed by the Talbot brothers, Sid Talbot (right) steering. By 1979 the barge had ceased to be used for bank repairs and was being used as a mooring pontoon at Arundel before being moved to Ford to be restored.

91.   Burpham Wharf was utilised for the carriage of chalk from the adjacent cliffs and for the dispatch of osiers. The building of the Mid-Sussex Railway in 1861 - 2 involved cutting a new channel at Offham to avoid the need for two swing bridges across the navigation. This resulted in the London to Arundel barges by-passing the wharf but local traffic continued until 1914 when this view was taken. (See also picture 107 in *West Sussex Waterways*.)

92.   Osiers, used for basket making, grew along the river bank and were stacked together with reeds for thatching, as seen in this 1910 view, awaiting dispatch to Arundel and London.

93. A sailing barge from Amberley approaches Arundel Castle in 1830. The eight foot tow-path between Houghton and Burpham begun in 1821 was not completed to Arundel until later in the century.

94. Henry Fox's water colour of horse towage is dated 1914. A steam tug, the *Jumna*, was used between Arundel and Littlehampton from 1856 to 1914 to assist vessels working up against the current.

95. Poling, sailing and the horse towage were employed by bargemen. The drawing (courtesy of the Tate Gallery) by J.M.W.Turner of the post-mill at Portreeves Acre above Arundel Castle shows a barge being poled downstream in about 1823. The mill was erected in 1769 and dismantled in 1864.

←——

96. The oil painting by Alfred East (1849 - 1913) shows casks being unloaded at a point very near to the Turner scene about sixty years later.

98. W.H.Mason's oil painting is of a barge being punted downstream towards Arundel Castle in 1864.

←——

97. Hay barges were not common on the Arun Navigation since hay was plentiful in the locality and there were few places nearby to which it could profitably be carried. This oil painting by Walter Caffyn, showing a hay raft lashed amidships, is dated 1878.

99.   Barques from North East England
regularly came up to Arundel Docks to
discharge cargoes of coal at the gasworks or to
the Co-operative Society Wharf to which the
left side boat is moored in this 1870s view.
Beyond the wharf stands the corn store which
finally housed a deck chair factory before
being gutted by fire in July 1930. It is now the
site of the present Town Quay.

100.   This 18th century flint and stone
warehouse by the wharf in Arundel in Arun
Street was recorded shortly before demolition
in 1970.

101. The steam tug *Jumma* can be seen moored above the schooner in about 1900. On arriving at the port it would sound its siren for all to hear.

102. Between 1861 and 1864 three windmills stood on the river bank at Arundel. Tower Mill was built in 1861 and destroyed by fire in 1892. It was initially a flour, but later a cement mill, which stood some 150 yards above the post mill at Portreeves Acre.

103. South Marshes Mill, built in 1840, ceased work after storm damage in 1915. The tower alone still stands.

104. An early nineteenth century view shows shipping approaching Arundel from Tortington Priory. The XIIth century priory had fallen into decay by the XVIIth century but the barn still exists.

ARUN NAVIGATION.

NEWBRIDGE WHARF.

NOTICE

IS HEREBY GIVEN, THAT

ON AND AFTER THE 1st OF APRIL, 1874,

THE

ARUN NAVIGATION PROPRIETORS

Will cease to be Wharfingers or receive or deliver Goods at **NEWBRIDGE WHARF**, in the Parish of Wisbro' Green, or be answerable for any Goods deposited there; the Wharf may, however, still be used at the risk of the Persons using the same.

Dated this 1st day of December, 1873.

(BY ORDER)

EDWARD ARNOLD,

CLERK TO THE PROPRIETORS.

PULLINGER, PRINTER, NORTH STREET, CHICHESTER.

105. In spite of determined opposition from the Arun Navigation Proprietors, the London & Brighton Railway Company obtained its Act in 1844 to build a line from Shoreham to Chichester which involved building this drawbridge across the Arun at Ford. The telescopic bridge had a sixty foot opening which took two men and a boy at least five minutes to open. Delays in opening the bridge to river traffic led to claims for compensation. £5 was the usual compensation paid for a 45 minute hold-up but in April 1858 a delay of 1 hour 50 minutes to the steam tug and her tow, the brigantine *Arun* resulted in £10 being paid.

106. Ford Railway Bridge was photographed in 1910.

107. In 1862 the single track timber drawbridge was replaced by this double track lift and roll iron structure. Although this had a centre span of 90 feet, the width of the navigable passage was reduced to 40 feet. This bridge took half an hour or so to open as all the wires passing over had to be disconnected. Strengthened in 1898, it remained substantially unaltered until it was replaced by a fixed bridge in 1938 when the railway was electrified.

108. The men who opened Ford bridge lived in the house on the right bank until 1938. By 1953 the house seen in this view had lost its roof and it was demolished soon afterwards.

PORTSMOUTH & ARUNDEL
CANAL NAVIGATION

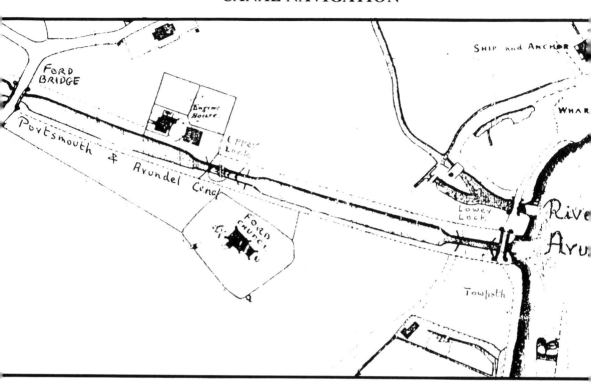

109.   The entrance to the Portsmouth & Arundel Canal at Ford, is seen in about 1840. The Upper (or second) lock is visible below the bridge which carried the road from Ford to Clymping. The pumping station housed a steam engine capable of lifting 96 hogsheads (5,000 gallons) of water a minute from the Arun. This rate was necessary as water could only be taken from the river from two hours after high water until one hour after low water, to prevent salt water entering the canal.

The Portsmouth & Arundel Canal Navigation linked the Arun Navigation at Ford to Portsmouth and was in four sections:

(i)   Barge canal from Ford to Hunston (9 miles). 2 locks.
(ii)   The Chichester Ship Canal (4 miles) from Birdham to Southgate Basin for 100 ton craft. 2 locks.
(iii) 13 miles of dredged channel from Birdham round the north coast of Hayling and Thorney Islands and across Langstone Harbour to Milton.
(iv)   The Portsea Ship Canal (2 miles) from Milton to the terminal basin at Halfway Houses capable of admitting 150 ton Craft. 2 locks. Opened in 1822 it ceased to be used after 1825 due to salt water polluting the water supplies. In 1831 the tidal channel round Portsea Island, Portcreek, was dredged to provide a direct link to Portsmouth Harbour.

The Navigation was completed in 1823 at a cost of £170,000 but now that the Napoleonic wars were over, trade suffered from competition with the coasting trade; furthermore the inland water route was circuitous and tedious. There were 52 locks between Portsmouth and London Bridge, tricky tidal channels, low bridges and often either too much or too little water. The opening of the railway to Chichester in 1846 caused the barge canal to become moribund and it was last used in 1856.

110. A closer view of the engine house at Ford was drawn in around 1860. The steam pumps were built over a well which was fed by a brick drain from the river to the tail of the lock. The pumps began operation on 12 August 1819 and probably ceased to be used about 1850. The two cottages adjacent to the engine house were built for the engineer and his assistant, who also acted as lock-keeper. The exact date when this water-colour was painted remains uncertain. Although the canal bed is dry and the paddle of the right hand lock gate is drawn, the gate itself seems in good condition and probably no more than five years had passed since the channel was drained. The engine house was demolished between 1876 when it is shown on the Ordnance survey and 1896, the year of the revised survey, by which date the locks had also been dismantled.

111. A view of the dried up bed at Ford. Only a change in levels denotes the site of the two locks. Adjacent to the house on the right bank built on the site of the two cottages, is one of the original small outhouses. Of the engine house there is no trace.

112. A northward view at the end in the Chichester Ship Canal at Hunston on 31 August 1994 includes the new bridge which replaced the Poyntz swing bridge. That historic structure is now on view near Southgate Basin. Richard Mitchell is removing weed from the screw of his recently completed self-built steam launch *Jastelle* and is moored close to the point where the canal from Ford once joined the present waterway.

The lower lock gates of Casher Lock, Birdham remained in place until the 1930s as this 1932 drawing shows. In the 1830s Edward Casher (he was Mayor of Portsmouth in 1843) had owned a Portsmouth fly barge which was used for carrying bullion to Queenhithe whence it was carted to the Bank of England.

113. Houseboats now line the lower reaches of the Chichester Ship Canal between Casher and Salterns Lock, Birdham. Two road bridges currently thwart the Chichester Canal Society's plan to gain access to the sea.

114. Salterns Lock leads into the tidal channel through which barges were formerly towed by tug round Thorney and Hayling islands. The lock was last used by commercial traffic in 1906 but was restored in 1932 by Chichester Yacht Company who used the canal above the lock for winter moorings.

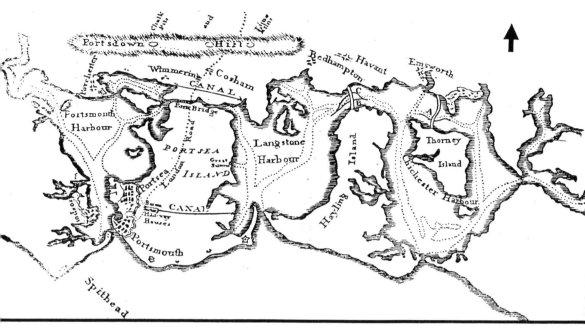

The dotted lines on John Rennie's plan of 1815 shows the navigable channels from Chichester Harbour round Thorney and Hayling islands to Langstone Harbour and the entrance to the Portsea Canal at Milton. The Cosham Canal was never built.

115. Two sailing barges *Langstone* and *Gladys* lie alongside Langstone Quay in about 1910. These barges were mainly used for transporting sand and gravel from Chichester Harbour to the quay where they were loaded on to horse drawn carts or railway wagons.

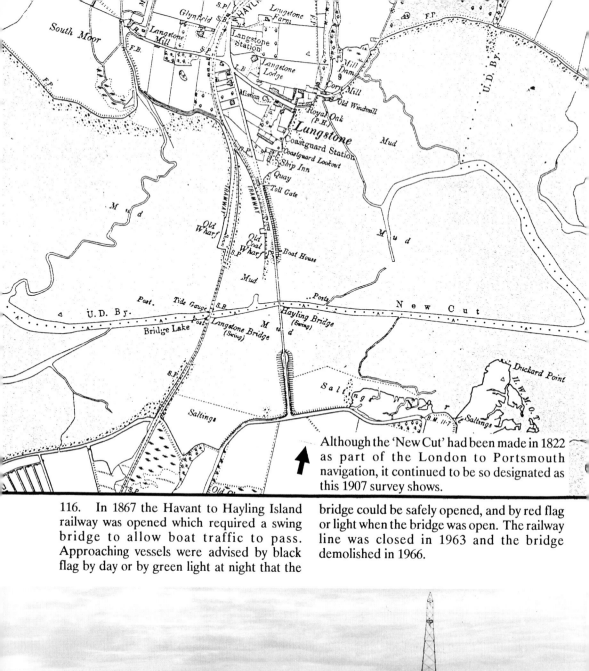

Although the 'New Cut' had been made in 1822 as part of the London to Portsmouth navigation, it continued to be so designated as this 1907 survey shows.

116. In 1867 the Havant to Hayling Island railway was opened which required a swing bridge to allow boat traffic to pass. Approaching vessels were advised by black flag by day or by green light at night that the bridge could be safely opened, and by red flag or light when the bridge was open. The railway line was closed in 1963 and the bridge demolished in 1966.

MILTON TO PORTSEA

The Portsea canal completed the final link in the chain of inland waterways between London and Portsmouth. It formed part of the Portsmouth & Arundel Canal Navigation which was built to enable barges to pass from the River Arun at Ford to Chichester Harbour from which point a dredged channel, marked by buoys, led round Thorney and Hayling islands to the entrance of the Portsea Canal in Langstone Harbour. The canal was dug 2 1/2 miles from Milton to Halfway Houses in the centre of Portsmouth. Its dimensions were those of a small ship canal to allow its use by coasting vessels of up to 150 tons burthen. The opening took place on 19 September 1822 but it was not long before local people were complaining that the wells which provided their drinking water were being contaminated by the salt water which had to be pumped into the canal. There were no funds available to overcome the problem. Traffic ceased in 1825. When John Rennie viewed the canal in July 1827 he observed that there was no water in it and it was indeed never used again. A further Act of Parliament enabled a new cut to be dredged across the neck of Portsea Island in 1830 to allow barges to load and unload from vessels in Portsmouth Harbour. However in spite of toll concessions being allowed by the other navigations (Wey, Godalming, Wey & Arun, Arun) and strenuous effort made to develop the London traffic, traders could not be persuaded to send their merchandise by inland waterway. They considered the shipping hazards of the North Foreland less of a problem than the heavy lockage involved (52 locks), the delays caused by ice, floods or drought and the greater risk of pilferage. Only a war with France could have saved the canal company from financial ruin. It cost £170,000 to build but its annual revenue never exceeded £1100 and it never paid a dividend. The basin at Halfway Houses was filled in in 1829 to form Arundel Street. Allders department store now stands on the site. The canal bed at Fratton was used for the track of the Portsmouth railway line opened in 1847. It was not, however, until 1896 that the company was finally wound up and most of the remainder of the canal levelled and turned into what is now Goldsmith Avenue and Locksway (formerly Asylum) Road.

117. This is the western shore of Langstone Harbour, looking east in 1967. Two lines of caravans mark the filled in bed of the Portsea canal where there are still traces of an embankment on each side.

118. The upper gates of Sea Lock Milton are seen in about 1900 with Lime Kiln cottages (on the right) which were demolished in the 1960s. A Portsmouth Guide of 1828 stated that "the banks of the canal afford a pleasant walk through the prolific gardens and highly cultivated fields, and which may be continually varied from the number of bridges which intersect it".

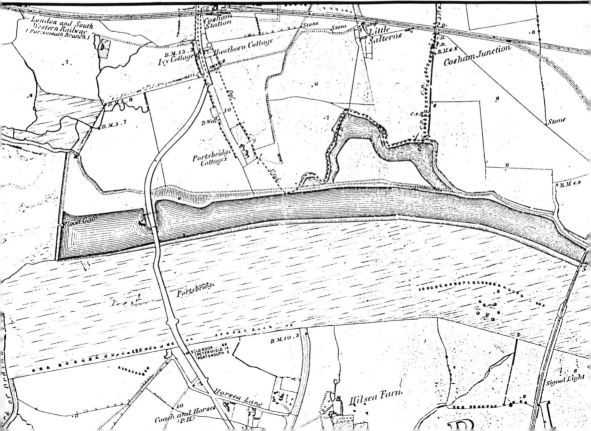

Enlarged PLAN of the Intended CANAL and BASINS at PORTSEA

to London

Half-way Houses

PORTSEA

from Portsmouth

BASIN

Church Path

BASIN

CANAL

Borough of Portsmouth

1815

Links 100   0 1 2 3 4 5 6 7 8 9 10 11 12 13 14 15 Chains

LANGSTONE HARBOUR TO
PORTSMOUTH HARBOUR

From 1830 until 1836 barge traffic passed to the north of Portsea Island along Portcreek. Portsmouth being an important naval base, the southern bank of Portcreek had to be maintained as a defence work. The London to Portsmouth barge traffic ceased in 1838 and as the navigation company was insolvent and unable to continue dredging, the Board of

It was intended that two basins should be built at the terminus of the Portsea Canal but in fact only one was built. Although opened in 1822, it was not used after 1825. The site of the canal on the right is now occupied by the railway. The main street on the left is now Commercial Road.

119. The early 1930s photograph shows the height of the south embankment of Portcreek.

Ordnance built embankments across the channel with flood gates to improve its defence potential at low tide, as seen in this 1859 survey, at 6" to 1 mile.

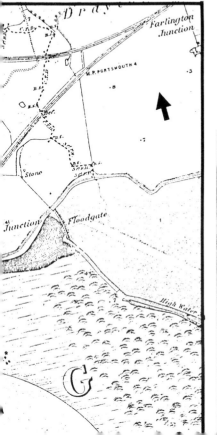
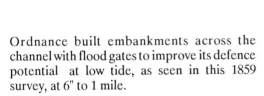

120. The problem of keeping Portcreek open for navigation can be judged by its present state at low tide. The navigation channel required constant dredging which the canal company ceased to do after the 1830s. This recent view shows the railway bridge which initially was of timber. It was replaced by an iron draw bridge in 1909 and became fixed in 1920. Attempts to revive trade between London and Portsmouth were restarted in 1830 following the completion of the Portcreek Cut.

MP Middleton Press

Easebourne Lane, Midhurst. West Sussex. GU29 9AZ   Tel: (0730) 813169 Fax: (0730) 812601
..... Write or telephone for our latest list .....

BRANCH LINES

Branch Line to Allhallows
Branch Lines to Alton
Branch Lines tround Ascot
Branch Line to Bude
Branch Lines to East Grinstead
Branch Lines tround Effingham Jn
Branch Lines to Exmouth
Branch Line to Fairford
Branch Lines around Gosport
Branch Line to Hawkhurst
Branch Line to Hayling
Branch Lines to Horsham
Branch Lines around Huntingdon
Branch Lines to Ilfracombe
Branch Lines to Longmoor
Branch Line to Lyme Regis
Branch Line to Lynton
Branch Lines around March
Branch Lines around Midhurst
Branch Line to Minehead
Branch Lines to Newport
Branch Lines around Portmadoc 1923-46
Branch Lines around Porthmadog 1954-94
Branch Lines to Seaton & Sidmouth
Branch Line to Selsey
Branch Lines around Sheerness
Branch Line to Shrewsbury
Branch Line to Southwold
Branch Line to Swanage
Branch Line to Tenterden
Branch Lines to Torrington
Branch Lines to Tunbridge Wells
Branch Lines tround Weymouth
Branch Lines around Wimborne

LONDON SUBURBAN RAILWAYS

Caterham and Tattenham Corner
Charing Cross to Dartford
Crystal Palace and Catford Loop
Holborn Viaduct to Lewisham
Kingston and Hounslow Loops
Lewisham to Dartford
London Bridge to Addiscombe
Mitcham Junction Lines
West Croydon to Epsom

STEAMING THROUGH

Steaming through Cornwall
Steaming through East Sussex
Steaming through the Isle of Wight
Steaming through Surrey
Steaming through West Hants
Steaming through West Sussex

SOUTH COAST RAILWAYS

Ashford to Dover
Bournemouth to Weymouth
Brighton to Eastbourne
Brighton to Worthing
Chichester to Portsmouth
Dover to Ramsgate
Eastbourne to Hastings
Hastings to Ashford
Ryde to Ventnor
Southampton to Bournemouth

SOUTHERN MAIN LINES

Basingstoke to Salisbury
Bromley South to Rochester
Charing Cross to Orpington
Crawley to Littlehampton
Dartford to Sittingbourne
East Croydon to Three Bridges
Epsom to Horsham
Exeter to Barnstaple
Faversham to Dover
Haywards Heath to Seaford
London Bridge to East Croydon
Orpington to Tonbridge
Salisbury to Yeovil
Sittingbourne to Ramsgate
Three Bridges to Brighton
Tonbridge to Hastings
Victoria to Bromley South
Waterloo to Windsor
Waterloo to Woking
Woking to Southampton
Yeovil to Exeter

COUNTRY RAILWAY ROUTES

Andover to Southampton
Bath To Evercreech Junction
Bournemouth to Evercreech Jn
Burnham to Evercreech Junction
East Kent Light Railway
Fareham to Salisbury
Guildford to Redhill
Reading to Basingstoke
Reading to Guildford
Redhill to Ashford
Strood to Paddock Wood
Woking to Alton

SOUTHERN RAILWAY VIDEO

War on the Line

TRAMWAY CLASSICS

Brighton's Tramways
Camberwell & W. Norwood Tramways
Dover's Tramways
Exeter & Taunton Tramways
Greenwich & Dartford Tramways
Hastings Tramways
Lewisham & Catford Tramways
Maidstone & Chatham
Southampton Tramways
Southend-on-sea Tramways
Thanet's Tramways

BUS BOOKS

Eastbourne Bus Story
Tillingbourne Bus Story

OTHER RAILWAY BOOKS

Garraway Father & Son
Industrial Railways of the South East
London Chatham & Dover Railway
South Eastern Railway
War on the Line

MILITARY BOOKS

Battle Over Portsmouth
Battle Over Sussex 1940
Blitz Over Sussex 1941-42
Military Defence of West Sussex

WATERWAY ALBUMS

Hampshire Waterways
Kent and East Sussex Waterways
London to Portsmouth Waterway
West Sussex Waterways

COUNTRY BOOKS

Brickmaking in Sussex
East Grinstead Then and Now
Leigh Park
Walking Ashdown Forest